ANSWERS *from the*
FOUNDING FATHERS

ANSWERS *from the* FOUNDING FATHERS

JERRY NEWCOMBE, D.Min.

TRUTH IN *Action* MINISTRIES™

Formerly
CORAL RIDGE MINISTRIES

Fort Lauderdale, Florida

Answers From The Founding Fathers
Jerry Newcombe, D. Min.
© 2011 Truth in Action Ministries

All Scriptures, unless otherwise noted, are taken from the New King James
Version. Copyright © 1982 by Thomas Nelson, Inc. Used by permission.
All rights reserved.

Scripture quotations marked (NIV) are taken from the Holy Bible, New
International Version®, NIV®. Copyright © 1973, 1978, 1984 by Biblica,
Inc.™ Used by permission of Zondervan. All rights reserved worldwide.
www.zondervan.com

Scripture quotations marked (ESV) are from The Holy Bible, English
Standard Version® (ESV®), copyright © 2001 by Crossway, a publishing
ministry of Good News Publishers. Used by permission. All rights reserved.

ISBN: 978-1-929626-07-6

Truth in Action Ministries
P.O. Box 1
Fort Lauderdale, FL 33302
1-800-988-7884
letters@tiam.org
www.TruthInAction.org

CONTENTS

Unique In History

Something unique happened in America.

Daniel Webster spoke of it in his 4th of July Oration in Fryeburg, Maine, 1802:

> We live under the only government that ever existed which was framed by . . . deliberate consultations of the people. Miracles do not cluster. That which has happened but once in 6,000 years cannot be expected to happen often. Such a government, once gone, might leave a void, to be filled, for ages, with revolution and tumult, riot and despotism.

James Wilson, a signer of the Declaration and Constitution, and a Supreme Court Justice appointed by George Washington, acknowledged at Pennsylvania's Ratifying Convention, November 26, 1787:

> After a period of 6,000 years has elapsed since the creation, the United States exhibit to the world the first instance . . . of a nation . . . assembling voluntarily . . . and deciding calmly concerning that system of government under which they . . . and their posterity should live.

Ronald Reagan concurred in a speech recorded for the American Medical Association's Operation Coffeecup Campaign, 1961:

> In this country of ours, took place the greatest revolution that has ever taken place in world's history. . . Every other revolution simply exchanged one set of rulers for another.
>
> But here for the first time in all the thousands of years of man's relation to man, a little group of the men, the founding fathers—for the first time—established the idea that you and I had within ourselves the God given right and ability to determine our own destiny.

What was so unique about America's founding?

What was the secret ingredient that made America's experiment of self-government work?

When the "Iron Curtain" and Berlin Wall came down, the U.S.S.R. was dismantled and the former Soviet States set up democratic republics. Twenty years have gone by and who now controls these former Soviet States?

By all indications, it is the black market and organized crime!

Why did the citizens of these former Soviet States not experience the same burst of freedom and opportunity that Americans experienced?

Could it have something to do with the fact they had seventy years of atheism underlying their experiment of the people ruling themselves?

When Middle East dictators are thrown out and democracies are set up, why do those countries inevitably get taken over by aggressive, violent Muslim Brotherhood leaders who institute Sharia Law and relegate non-Muslims and women to a second-class status?

Why do the citizens of those countries not experience the same liberties and equalities that America's citizens experience?

Could it have something to do with the fact they have Islam underlying their experiment of the people ruling themselves, and Islam's Sharia Law has no concept of equality?

What was the mysterious variable in the equation of America's founding that gave citizens of this country the most freedom, opportunity and prosperity of any nation that ever existed in all the 6,000 years of recorded human history?

Dr. Jerry Newcombe reveals the secret ingredient in this intriguing book, *Answers from the Founding Fathers.* What is the source of our rights? Are religion and morality indispensable supports? Why is it important to have a limited government—"of the people, by the people and for the people"? What is the role of education and the courts? How is economic prosperity achieved? What is the origin of religious liberty? Why did the founders emphasize prayer?

Dr. Newcombe delves into the principle of *self-government,* how a country can get by with few external laws if the people live by an internal law.

There is a Christian component to the settling and founding of America that has made her great. But a land born in great part for religious freedom is fast becoming a land where religious freedom is at risk.

Modern secularists have rewritten history and spread a false message about our founders and their intent when it comes to religion. As a student of American history, I am positive that our founders intended Christianity to flourish, even in the public square, but not in a compulsory way. What we find today is that groups like the ACLU are now essentially imposing atheism on the public square—in a compulsory way.

Our founders didn't want the ACLU version of the First Amendment. In the ACLU's version, they want to get God out of everything. That's not what the founders wanted. The founders simply didn't want the European version of church-state relations, where you had the king choosing a state denomination. England had the state Anglican Church. In Germany it was a state Lutheran Church, with other parts being Catholic. In Switzerland, it was the Calvinist denomination. Italy, Spain, and France were Roman Catholic. In Greece and Russia it was Eastern Orthodox.

But in no way did our founders want to remove God from every facet of life. Recognizing God went beyond the founding era. At some point in their history, each of the 50 States mentioned God in their State Constitutions.

Because of the prevalence of views like those espoused (and forced in lawsuits) by groups such as the ACLU, the freedoms we have in our country are being taken away. We're seeing a displacement of the principles that made our country what it is (was), and we're seeing new principles put in. Calvin Coolidge said, "You can't have the results, if you neglect the cause." You can't have the results of freedom if we neglect the cause, the Judeo-Christian values that gave us this country.

I once put together a book called *Three Secular Reasons Why America Should be Under God*. These are secular reasons. The first one is: Do you like having rights the government can't take away. I've talked to atheists and they say, "Yeah, I like having rights the government can't take away."

Well, then, those rights have to come to you from a power higher than the government. That's why the Declaration of Independence says, "All men are endowed by their Creator with certain inalienable rights, and to secure these rights, governments are instituted among men."

Rights come from God; government's job is to protect those rights. But if there's no God, where do your rights come from? If there's no God, the rights come from the state, making the state the new god. Those rights can be taken away, and that's what you have in totalitarian countries. So, if you like having rights the government can't take away, you want those rights to come to you from a power higher than the government.

The second is: Do you like being equal? Someone might answer, "Certainly! And I'll sue you if you say I'm not equal." Where did the concept of equality come from? Did it come from Saudi Arabia where you face the death penalty if you convert from Islam to another religion? Did equality come from atheistic Communist China, where they're still arresting illegal house church leaders?

Harry S. Truman said in his Inaugural Address, "We believe all men are created equal, because we're created in the image of God." Again, if there's no God, who decides who's equal? The government? What if you get a Hitler in charge of the government and he decides that Jews aren't equal? Or you get a Stalin in charge of the government and he decides Ukrainians aren't equal, and he killed millions of them. Or a Muslim Caliph in charge of the government and he decides that non-Muslims and women are not equal. Or you get a Democrat appointed Supreme Court Justice like Roger Taney, who wrote in the *Dred Scott* case, "Slaves are so far inferior, they should be enslaved for their own benefit"—a clearly racist statement. Well, what we need is a standard of equality higher than whoever currently gets to sit in the seat of government. God, as the source of our rights, secures those rights.

And then, the third reason is: Do you like a country with a lot of laws or few laws? Well, everyone likes few laws, but in order for there to be order in society with few external laws, the populace has to have an internal law. That's why John Adams said in 1798, "Our Constitution was made only for a moral and religious people; it's totally inadequate for the government of any other."

In other words, our government was designed to govern people who could govern themselves. And the more internal restraints the populace had, the less external restraints they needed, and the greater their freedom.

But what's happened is: We've stripped away the internal restraints. We tell people, "Give in to your lusts and passions, and do whatever you want," and they do, and they commit crimes, and people say, "Government, do something!" So, the government puts in external restraints. And every new law that's passed is a bar that comes down on our cage, taking away some of our freedom. We've taken the Ten Commandments off the schoolroom walls; now we have to install more security in the schools. We've taken down God's commandment, "Thou shall not murder" because man is made in His image, and instead we teach little Johnny situation ethics, telling him that if there are too many people in the lifeboat, he has to decide which person is useless and shove that one over the side. Then he gets out in his neighborhood and decides some kid's useless and blows him away. Then we're shocked that he acted out the new philosophy that he was taught in the classroom, rather than the good old fashioned "Thou shall not murder" because man's made in the image of God.

What we're doing is: We're stripping away the internal Golden Rule. Think of that—"Do unto others, as you would have them do unto you." If everyone in the country had that internal belief in the Golden Rule, we wouldn't need any other laws. But what's happened is: We've now switched it out to "Whoever has the gold, rules." We're seeing people selfishly acting on that and chaos comes as a result. Now we need the government to come in and restore order by passing more and more and more laws. Every new law that's passed takes away another piece of our freedom, till pretty soon, we won't be a free country anymore.

So, if we like having a country with few laws, then we want the populace to have an internal law.

Of course, people say, "Well, why can't people just be ethical?" That sounds okay, until you realize that only a small percentage of the populace will be ethical for ethics' sake. William Linn, who was the first chaplain of the U.S. House, said, "Let my neighbor once persuade himself that there is no God, and he will soon pick my pocket and break, not only my leg, but my neck. If there be no God, laws are, simply, the ordinance of man only, and we cannot be subject to it for conscience sake."

If there's no God, laws are simply made up by men, and since I'm a man and you're a man, why should you have to obey the laws I made up, and why should I have to obey the laws you made up? Then it boils down to whoever winds up with the political and military power gets to force everyone else to obey his laws. That's the equivalent of the banana republics' military coups.

Our founders wanted to have a stable country, so they said in effect, "We have our laws based on a higher law, and that's God."

America has a wonderful foundation, laid by the founding fathers, based largely on principles found in the Bible. They have given us answers to help us get back on the right track. That's why I'm pleased to recommend this book by my friend, Dr. Jerry Newcombe.

Can the grand American experiment of people ruling themselves without a king continue?

Only if we learn the truths that are in Dr. Jerry Newcombe's book, *Answers from the Founding Fathers*. America's founders have given us the answers we need for modern America, if we would only heed them. Jerry has done a great job of assembling some of those key answers "for such a time as this."

WILLIAM J. FEDERER
Author and Compiler, *America's God and Country Encyclopedia of Quotations*

CHAPTER ONE

God Is The Source of Our Rights

*We hold these truths
to be self-evident, that all men are
created equal, that they are endowed
by their Creator with certain
unalienable Rights...*[1]

Thomas Jefferson,
Declaration of Independence, 1776

A majority of Americans recognize that as a nation we are off track. We are not headed in the right direction. But what direction should we go? Certainly not down the current path of national bankruptcy—financially, morally, and above all, spiritually.

We believe that if America is to survive as a nation, we need to return to some core principles that our founding fathers promoted. The purpose of this book is to listen to the founders themselves so that we may return to American greatness. It could very well be that America's best days are ahead of us, but certainly not if the present trends continue.

Is America still a special place? Are we still a great country? What made us so, and can we get it back? These are some of the questions we will attempt to answer in this book.

AN EXCELLENT FOUNDATION

What makes America so special? Why is it that would-be immigrants literally risk their lives to try and get here? Some will risk their lives to leave Cuba, going through shark-infested waters. But don't they know they have free health care there?

Why do people vote with their feet to try to get to this country? What makes the U.S. so special? The answer has to do with one simple fact: We have an excellent foundation—one that recognizes our rights come from God. Period. That's what our national birth certificate, the Declaration of Independence, says.

Even when America doesn't live up to its creed—that our Creator has endowed us with certain unalienable rights—it's still a good creed. As Dr. Martin Luther King, Jr., said in his classic speech at the Lincoln Memorial in 1963: "I still have a dream. It is a dream deeply rooted in the American dream. I have a dream that one day this nation will rise up and live out the true meaning of its creed: 'We hold these truths to be self-evident; that all men are created equal.'"[2]

I believe that what is best about America gets back to our Judeo-Christian heritage. I don't think there would be an America without the unique role the Bible played in the founding of our nation. Because America began as a Christian nation, people of all faiths or no faith are welcome here.

The Tea Party movement has been popular lately. The leader of the first tea party (the Boston Tea Party of December 1773) was Sam Adams—the lightning rod of the American Revolution. Without him, we might not have achieved independence, certainly not when we did. When Sam Adams was signing the Declaration of Independence, he made a positive reference about Jesus Christ, "We have this day restored the Sovereign to Whom all men ought to be obedient. He reigns in heaven and from the rising to the setting of the sun, let His kingdom come."[3]

Consider George Washington. In his Farewell Address, he noted: "Of all the dispositions and habits which lead to political prosperity, religion and morality are indispensable supports. In vain would that man claim the tribute of patriotism, who should labor to subvert these great pillars of human happiness.... Let it simply be asked where is the security for prosperity, for reputation, for life, if the sense of religious obligation desert the oaths, which are the instruments of investigation in the Courts of Justice? And let us with caution indulge the supposition, that morality can be maintained without religion. Whatever may be conceded to the influence of refined education on minds of peculiar structure, reason and experience both forbid us to expect that national morality can prevail in exclusion of religious principle."[4] When the founding fathers spoke of "religion," they were speaking of Christianity—in a nation which at the time was 99.8% professing Christian.[5]

BEFORE THE DECLARATION OF INDEPENDENCE

The Bible teaches that humankind has been made in the image of God. Because of that, we have value. Christianity spread this teaching—which ultimately came from the ancient Hebrews—expanded upon it and sent it out into the whole world.

Even within Christian countries, it took a long time for the implications of this great doctrine to work its way out slowly over the centuries. One of the great milestones in human history was the Magna Charta, (the great charter) of 1215, written by the head of the Church in England—Steven Langton, the Archbishop of Canterbury.

The context of the Magna Charta is that King John was acting like a tyrant, and his nobles were rebelling. As a peacemaker, Archbishop Langton proposed a written treaty between the ruler and his subjects.

This was a milestone in history. In his book, *History of the English People,* author John Richard Green notes that the Magna Charta "marks the transition from the age of traditional rights, preserved in the nation's memory...to the age of written legislation."[6]

Note how the Magna Charta acknowledges the Lord:

> John, by the grace of God, King of England, Lord of Ireland, Duke of Normandy, Aquitaine, and Count of Anjou, to his Archbishops, Bishops, Abbots, Earls, Barons, Justiciaries, Foresters...and his faithful subjects, greeting. Know ye, that we, in the presence of God, and for the salvation of our soul... and unto the honor of God and the advancement of Holy Church, and amendment of our Realm.... have, in the first place, granted to God, and by this our present Charter confirmed, for us and our heirs for ever:
>
> That the Church of England shall be free, and have her whole rights, and her liberties.... We also have granted to all the freemen of our kingdom for us and for our heirs for ever, all the underwritten liberties to be had and holden by them and their heirs, of us and our heirs for ever....[7]

The Magna Charta gave us the trial-by-jury system. The biblical worldview was at the heart of this great milestone in history, a milestone that I believe reached its zenith five-and-a-half centuries later in the American push for independence.

Another very important development in law that goes back to the Bible also occurred during the Middle Ages, and that was the idea of equality of all before the law. Joseph Reither, former history professor at New York University and author of *World History at a Glance,* writes:

> The ideal of human equality is a very new concept among men. It is derived from the Christian teaching reiterated throughout the Middle Ages that the souls of all men are of equal value in the sight of God.[8]

Thus, it was reserved to Christianity to teach the world that all men are created equal—even though it took a long time for Christians themselves to get that right.

In his book, *The Rise of the Republic of the United States,* written in 1890, author Richard Frothingham notes the link between Christianity and the idea that we are created equal:

> This low view of man was exerting its full influence when Rome was at the height of its power and glory. Christianity then appeared with its central doctrine, that man was created in the Divine image, was destined for immortality; pronouncing, that, in the eye of God, all men are equal. This asserted for the individual an independent value. It occasioned the great inference, that man is superior to the State, which ought to be fashioned for his use. This was the advent of a new spirit and a new power in the world.[9]

Christianity teaches that all of us are equal before the Cross. At the foot of the Cross of Christ, the only source for salvation, the rich, powerful man is no greater than the powerless slave.

The Reformation of the 16th century helped affirm more of the rights of man. For example, through the influence of Calvinism, the Dutch created a manifesto declaring their freedom from Spain on June 26, 1581, which said, "Every man knows that subjects are not created by God for princes, but princes for the sake of their subjects. If a prince endeavors to take from his subjects their old liberties, privileges, and customs, he must be considered not as a prince, but as a tyrant, and another prince may of right be chosen in his place as the head."[10] This kind of declaration was an important predecessor to the American Declaration of Independence.

ACTIONS AGAINST THE COLONIES

Jump ahead to the American colonies in the 1770s. At that time, the Americans had for two decades experienced one tyranny after another forced on them by a tyrannical king (and in some cases, Parliament). They patiently tried to make peace without compromising their God-given rights, but things became intolerable.

For example, Ben Franklin said to William Pitt (the Earl of Chatham), a British Parliamentary leader who favored the American cause, "I never heard from any person the least expression of a wish for a separation."[11] In October 1774, George Washington wrote: "No such thing as independence is desired by any thinking man in America."[12]

Thomas Jefferson says, in reference to the Battles of Lexington and Concord—clear examples of British aggression: "Before the nineteenth of April 1775, I never heard a whisper of a disposition to separate from Great Britain."[13] Around the same time in that same year, John Adams published in Boston: "That there are any who pant after independence, is the greatest slander on the province."[14]

As the first great historian of America, George Bancroft, who wrote the six-volume, monumental series, *A History of the United States* (final version, 1890), put it: "The American revolution grew out of the soul of the people, and was an inevitable result of a living affection for freedom, which set in motion harmonious effort as certainly as the beating of the heart sends warmth and color through the system."[15] The Americans cherished their God-given rights, and these rights were being systematically trampled upon. Each day was marching toward an inevitable breaking point.

George Bancroft notes that the American Congress,

feeling the squeeze of tyranny from the king, appealed to a higher source. Congress "had made its appeal to the King of kings."[16] Since the king was denying them their rights, Congress appealed to Jesus Christ, who overrules all human kings.

Similarly, the 2nd provincial congress of Massachusetts in 1775 declared to their fellow citizens of that state: "Resistance to tyranny becomes the Christian and social duty of each individual. Fleets, troops, and every implement of war are sent into the province, to wrest from you that freedom which it is your duty, even at the risk of your lives, to hand inviolate to posterity. Continue steadfast, and, with a proper sense of your dependence on God, nobly defend those rights which heaven gave, and no man ought to take from us."[17]

Christians were praying hard and even fasting over this brewing crisis, including members of Congress. For example, May 17, 1776, was declared a national day of fasting. Bancroft notes a worship service on that day attended by founding father John Adams: "George Duffield, the minister of the third Presbyterian church in Philadelphia, with John Adams for a listener, drew a parallel between George III and Pharaoh, and inferred that the same providence of God which had rescued the Israelites designed to free the Americans."[18]

At another point, John Adams had written to his wife, Abigail: "We are hastening rapidly to great events. Governments will be up everywhere before midsummer, and an end to royal style, titles, and authority. May God in his providence, overrule the mighty revolution for the good of mankind."[19]

The permanent break with Mother England was becoming inevitable. Soon it was to be put into writing.

THE DECLARATION OF INDEPENDENCE'S AUTHOR

The Declaration of Independence is a superb statement of the rights of man. As we'll see, it draws heavily from many Christian sources.

Of course, the chief author of the Declaration is Thomas Jefferson. He once expressed his natural reluctance to break from the Mother Country. Independence was not something to take lightly. He wrote, "There is not in the British empire a man who more cordially loves a union with Great Britain than I do; but, by the God that made me, I will cease to exist before I yield to a connection on such terms as the British parliament propose; and in this I speak the sentiments of America."[20]

Some people like to categorize Jefferson as a rank unbeliever. That is not accurate. Also it is not accurate in the least to say that he wanted to keep God or Christianity out of the public square. In a sense, these modern historical revisionists are indirectly arguing that the Declaration is the work of unbelief.

Sometimes, skeptics argue that Thomas Jefferson's alleged heterodoxy puts him clearly in the Unitarian camp (slightly before the rise of the official Unitarian movement). However, Mark Beliles, co-founder of the Providence Foundation, has done much research on Jefferson, back to many primary sources. He told me that it is accurate to say that Jefferson was not a good Anglican, but that does not necessarily mean he was not a good Christian.

Regardless of Jefferson's personal views on Christianity, look at his actions as president when it comes to the faith. This list is compiled through Dr. Beliles' research. Thomas Jefferson:

- Promoted legislative and military chaplains,
- Established a national seal using a biblical symbol,
- Included the word God in our national motto,
- Established official days of fasting and prayer—at least on the state level,
- Punished Sabbath breakers,
- Punished marriages contrary to biblical law,
- Punished irreverent soldiers,
- Protected the property of churches,
- Required that oaths be phrased by the words "So Help Me God" and be sworn on the Bible,
- Granted land to Christian churches to reach the Indians,
- Granted land to Christian schools,

- Allowed government property and facilities to be used for worship,
- Used the Bible and non-denominational religious instruction in the public schools. He was involved in three different school districts and the plan in each one of these required—*required*—that the Bible be taught in our public schools.
- Allowed clergymen to hold public office and encouraged them to do so,
- Funded religious books for public libraries,
- Funded salaries for missionaries,
- Funded the construction of church buildings for Indians,
- Exempted churches from taxation,
- Established professional schools of theology. He wanted to bring the entire faculty of Calvin's theological seminary over from Geneva, Switzerland, and establish them at the University of Virginia.
- Wrote treaties requiring other nations to guarantee religious freedom, including religious speeches and prayers in official ceremonies.[21]

And we shouldn't forget that when he was president, Jefferson attended church every week at the U.S. Capitol, exposing himself to evangelical preaching.

I'm tempted to add, with tongue in cheek—"Well, other than all that, he was a good atheist." As the late Dr. D. James Kennedy once put it, "My friends, the *real* Thomas Jefferson is the ACLU's worst nightmare."[22]

THE DECLARATION OF INDEPENDENCE

The adoption of the Declaration of Independence July 4th, 1776, marks our birth as a nation. This classic document says that our rights come from God. What God gives, the state cannot take away. Our rights are non-negotiable.

The Declaration states WHY we exist as a nation, as opposed

to the Constitution which spells out the HOW our government is to work.

The Declaration mentions God four times:

- ". . . the Laws of Nature and of Nature's God . . ."
- "all men are created equal, they are endowed by their Creator with certain unalienable rights . . ."
- ". . . appealing to the Supreme Judge of the World for the Rectitude of our Intentions . . ."
- ". . . with a firm Reliance on the Protection of Divine Providence . . ."[23]

If our rights came from the state, the state could withdraw them. That has happened repeatedly in the past, where a state, such as the Soviet Union, took over and removed God as the source of rights. You have no rights; you must obey the state. The last century was the bloodiest century in all of human history because of godless, totalitarian regimes.

Stalin has slain his millions; Mao his tens of millions. And it's all based on the idea that our rights come from the state, not from God.

It is no small thing that America was founded as one nation under God.

John F. Kennedy said in his Inaugural Address, "I am proud of the revolutionary beliefs for which our forebears fought . . . the belief that the rights of man come not from the generosity of the state but the hands of God."[24]

DRAWING FROM CHRISTIAN SOURCES

Much of the Declaration of Independence deals with more than two dozen charges against King George III for his tyranny against the American colonists. Dr. Donald S. Lutz, a great scholar on American constitutionalism, noted that most of the charges were virtually copied and pasted from South Carolina's 1776 Constitution, which ends with the words "So help me God." Dr. Lutz states, "South Carolina's list contained nineteen of the Declaration's twenty-eight charges."[25]

The gist of the charges is that the colonists should be enjoying their God-given rights as British citizens, but instead, the king is trampling on those rights—one after another. Because George III had so abused their rights, he was no longer fit to be recognized as their king. This idea echoes what a Boston minister had said a decade or so earlier.

Rev. Jonathan Mayhew, minister of West Church, Boston, declared the following in 1765 in a sermon upon hearing of King George's Stamp Act:

> The king is as much bound by his oath not to infringe the legal rights of the people, as the people are bound to yield subjection to him. From whence it follows that as soon as the prince sets himself above the law, he loses the king in the tyrant. He does, to all intents and purposes, un-king himself.[26]

After his laundry list of the monarch's abuses in the Declaration, Jefferson concludes, "In every stage of these oppressions we have petitioned for redress in the most humble terms: our repeated petitions have been answered only by repeated injury. A prince, whose character is thus marked by every act which may define a tyrant, is unfit to be the ruler of a free people."[27]

A GREAT DEAL OF INPUT

When Thomas Jefferson wrote the Declaration of Independence, he did so with a great deal of input from those who had gone before him. He did a masterful job of setting forth our nation's reasons for coming into being, but his thoughts were not original. As Donald S. Lutz, author of *The Origins of American Constitutionalism*, points out: "[T]here was nothing new in the phrasing and ideas of the Declaration."[28]

Some of Jefferson's ideas came from John Locke, who wrote the classic *Second Treatise on Government*, which derives many of its arguments by appealing to the Bible. Locke argues against the divine right of kings in favor of the will of the people. Locke was a Christian, who promoted study of the Scriptures. He said, "...because the Christian religion is a revelation from God Almighty, which is contained in the Bible; and so all the knowledge we can have of it must be derived from thence."[29]

Locke often writes of the rights of "life, liberty, and property." Locke is sometimes categorized as an unbeliever. But he wrote a book of apologetics of the faith, *The Reasonableness of Christianity*.

Dr. Donald S. Lutz points out: "John Locke on natural rights supported both God's will as revealed in the Bible and the traditional guarantees of Magna Carta and the common law."[30]

How did most people during the founding era even know about John Locke and his political philosophy? Through Christian sermons. Dr. Lutz says, "It is a little-appreciated irony that the primary avenue for the introduction of Locke's thinking into colonial and revolutionary America was through election-day sermons by the clergy."[31]

Sir William Blackstone, the noted 18th century British jurist, said that as men obey God, they pursue happiness:

> In consequence of which mutual connection of justice and human felicity, he has not perplexed the law of nature with a multitude of abstracted rules and precepts, referring merely to the fitness or unfitness of things, as some have vainly surmised; but has graciously reduced the rule of obedience to this one paternal precept, "that man should pursue his own happiness." This is the foundation of what we call ethics, or natural law.[32]

The "pursuit of happiness"—words made famous by the Declaration of Independence—originally meant obedience to God. Jefferson, like other founding fathers, including James Madison, read and admired Blackstone's *Commentaries*.

Sir William Blackstone said that God has revealed Himself

both in nature (in His creation) and through the Scriptures. The Declaration's reference to "the laws of nature and of nature's God" reflects this concept. This idea is at least 3,000 years old, in that it can be seen in Psalm 19, wherein David extols God for His creation and for His revealed law, His Word.

PRESBYTERIAN INFLUENCE

During the first part of the 18th century, British persecution of Scottish Presbyterians in Scotland and Ireland caused *hundreds of thousands* of Presbyterians to emigrate to the American colonies. In a nation of three million (at the time of Independence), hundreds of thousands of people is significant. This persecution by the British against the Scots would soon come back to haunt the British.

The Scots (and the Presbyterians) played a key role in America's push for Independence. Dr. Marshall Foster, of the World History Institute, leads many tours showing the Christian roots of America. Foster points out, "About one-fourth of the colonists were Scotch-Irish Presbyterians, and they made up about 80% of George Washington's Officer Corps, and about 50% of his army. And those Scots knew how to hate the English, ever since the days of William Wallace. So, you know why we won the Revolution—there's one of the biggest reasons."[33]

Historian George Bancroft labeled the American War for Independence as a Presbyterian phenomenon:

> The Revolution of 1776, so far as it was affected by religion was a Presbyterian measure. It was the natural outgrowth of the principles which the Presbyterianism of the Old World planted in her sons, the English Puritans, the Scotch Covenanters, the French Huguenots, the Dutch Calvinists, and the Presbyterians of Ulster.[34]

During the Revolutionary War, the British Prime Minister, Horace Walpole, remarked to Parliament, "Cousin America has run off with a Presbyterian parson."[35] That Presbyterian "parson" was Rev. John Witherspoon, the president of Princeton—a signer of the Declaration of Independence as a delegate from New Jersey.

Even before the war, a group of Presbyterians pushed for a break from England. More than a year before the United States was officially born on July 4, 1776, with the Declaration of Independence, 27 Presbyterian elders of Scotch-Irish origin, who lived in Mecklenburg, North Carolina, and were led by Elder Ephraim Brevard, decided to declare their own independence from Great Britain. Brevard was a Princeton graduate who had studied under Witherspoon.

In May 1775, as the Second Continental Congress was meeting (again, a full year before the Third Continental Congress declared independence), these brave Presbyterians declared independence in a series of short resolves. Some of the exact wording of their resolves made it into the Declaration of Independence.

George Bancroft reports: "The resolves were transmitted with all speed . . . to the British government."[36] They were then sent by courier to the Continental Congress in Philadelphia. Dr. Loraine Boettner, a scholar who has been quoted by the Supreme Court, says of this declaration by the Presbyterian elders: "It was the fresh, hearty greeting of the Scotch-Irish to their struggling brethren in the North, and their bold challenge to the power of England."[37]

Here is what the Presbyterian elders of North Carolina resolved on May 20, 1775, as they declared independence from "the Crown of Great Britain." See if any of it sounds familiar:

> That we do hereby declare ourselves a free and independent people; are, and of right ought to be a sovereign and self-governing association, under the control of no power, other than that of our God and the General Government of the Congress: To the maintainance of which Independence we solemnly pledge to each other our mutual co-operation, our Lives, our Fortunes, and our most Sacred Honor.[38]

Now, here are portions of the actual Declaration of Independence (written more than a year later):

> We, therefore, the representatives of the United States of America, in General Congress, assembled, appealing to the Supreme Judge of the world for the rectitude of our intentions...declare that these united colonies are, and of right ought to be free and independent states; that they are absolved from all allegiance to the British Crown...And for the support of this declaration, with a firm reliance on the protection of Divine Providence, we mutually pledge to each other our lives, our fortunes and our sacred honor.[39]

Was Jefferson guilty of plagiarism? No, we should not anachronistically accuse him of violating copyright laws that were to come into existence about a century or more later. Author N. S. McFetridge notes that there is historical evidence that Jefferson did borrow from the Presbyterian document:

> In correcting his first draft of the Declaration it can be seen, in at least a few places, that Jefferson has erased the original words and inserted those which are first found in the Mecklenburg Declaration. No one can doubt that Jefferson had Brevard's resolutions before him when he was writing his immortal Declaration.[40]

GOD-GIVEN RIGHTS

Thus, we see that Jefferson and the founders declared that our rights come from God. They drew on primarily Christian sources to make such a declaration.

Because of the adoption of the Declaration of Independence in July 1776, John Adams would write that this day "will be the most memorable epoch in the history of America; to be celebrated by succeeding generations as the great anniversary festival, commemorated as the day of deliverance, by solemn acts of devotion to God Almighty, from one end of the continent to the other, from this time forward forevermore."[41]

The idea that our rights come from God would appear to be a universal sentiment among the founding fathers. One of the signers of the Declaration of Independence and of the Constitution was James Wilson, who was appointed to the first Supreme Court by George Washington. Justice Wilson served there for about a decade.

He delivered Lectures on Law at the College of Philadelphia from 1789 through 1791, wherein he declared the divine origin of law. He said:

> That law, which God has made for man in his present state; that law, which is communicated to us by reason and conscience, the divine monitors within us, and by the sacred oracles, the divine monitors without us. . . .
>
> As promulgated by reason and the moral sense it has been called natural; as promulgated by the holy scriptures, it has been called revealed law. . . .
>
> But it should always be remembered, that this law, natural or revealed, made for men or for nations, flows from the same divine source; it is the law of God. . . .[42]

"THE GENERAL PRINCIPLES OF CHRISTIANITY"

In 1813, John Adams wrote to Thomas Jefferson, "The general Principles, on which the Fathers Achieved Independence, were the only Principles in which that beautiful Assembly of young Gentlemen could Unite, and these Principles only could be intended by them in their Address, or by me in my Answer. And what were these general Principles? I answer, the general Principles of Christianity, in which all those Sects were united: And the general Principles of English and American Liberty, in which all those young Men United, and which had United all Parties in America, in Majorities sufficient to assert and maintain her Independence."[43]

If that isn't politically incorrect enough, John Adams goes on to assert that Christianity, and not any other philosophy or religious system, gave birth to our freedom:

> Now I will avow, that I then believed, and now believe, that those general Principles of Christianity, are as eternal and immutable, as the Existence and Attributes of God; and that those Principles of Liberty, are as unalterable as human Nature and our terrestrial, mundane System. I could therefore safely say, consistently with all my then and present Information, that I believed they would never make Discoveries in contradiction to these general Principles. In favour of these general Principles in Phylosophy, Religion and Government, I could fill Sheets of quotations from Frederick of Prussia, from Hume, Gibbon, Bolingbroke, Reausseau and Voltaire, as well as Neuton and Locke: not to mention thousands of Divines and Philosophers of inferiour Fame.[44]

CONCLUSION

The founders weren't perfect, and they didn't create a perfect government, but it is sure greater than the alternatives. And the Constitution they gave us can be amended if needs be—as it was, for example, to correct the evils of slavery in the 13th and 14th Amendments—after some 600,000 men lost their lives in the Civil War. As David Gibbs, Jr. points out, the Constitution is not like the Bible—which never needs to be amended.

At the time of the founding of America, again, 99.8% of Americans were professing Christians. Their political philosophy grew out of the Judeo-Christian tradition.

The pulpits of New England preached forth liberty—liberty beginning with the liberty of the individual soul set free by the power of God—because Jesus died for sinners and rose again. That spiritual freedom gave birth to political freedom for all, regardless of creed.

In short, America is and never was perfect—far from it— but the founders got some things right—our rights come from God, so they're non-negotiable. It is the duty of government to honor those God-give rights.

We should always remember what Ronald Reagan once said, "America needs God more than God needs America. If we ever forget that we are 'One Nation Under God,' then we will be a nation gone under."[45]

CHAPTER TWO

Providence
and Independence

*No people can be bound to acknowledge
and adore the invisible hand which conducts the
affairs of men more than those of the united states.
every step by which they have advanced to the
character of an independent nation seems to
have been distinguished by some token
of providential agency....*[46]

George Washington,
First Inaugural Address

Many of the founders echoed the sentiment Washington expressed at his inauguration when he said that we Americans should be grateful to God for helping us become an independent nation. They, along with Washington, believed that God's hand had helped establish this nation as a sovereign nation. We need to rediscover that truth in our day.

In this chapter, we want to explore some of the difficult steps the founders took to try to prevent war, at virtually all costs—except the jettisoning of their God-given liberties. Since God is at work in history, often behind the scenes, often undetected by human beings, it's easy to conclude—as did George Washington—that it was the will of God for our nation to come into being.

A LESSON FROM OUR MONEY

The view that God's hand helped create and sustain this nation can actually be seen by a review of much of our money— all of which declares "In God we trust." Stephen McDowell, co-founder of the Providence Foundation, explains: "You pull out your dollar you see George Washington's picture, the father of our country who is a Christian man who reflected it in his actions and in his words."[47]

As we have seen, during his first Inaugural Address, Washington said, "No people can be bound to acknowledge and adore the Invisible Hand which conducts the affairs of men more than those of the United States. Every step by which they have advanced to the character of an independent nation seems to have been distinguished by some token of providential agency...."[48]

Take that same dollar bill and look on the other side, and we see (on the left) in Latin this phrase—*Annuit coeptis*, meaning, "He has favored our undertakings." As Stephen McDowell notes, "God has blessed our undertakings because the founders believed that God and His providence had overseen the birth of this nation and that is reflected there....There are many miracles God did during the American Revolution, but the greatest miracle was that 13 sovereign, independent states could gather together to unite to work together as one. John Adams said it was like making 13 clocks strike together in unison."[49]

Go back to the wallet and pull out a five dollar bill, and we see Abraham Lincoln. During the dark days of the Civil War, our 16th president called for a national day of fasting and prayer. He reminded the nation: "We have been the recipients of the choicest bounties of Heaven. We have been preserved, these many years, in peace and prosperity. We have grown in numbers, wealth and power, as no other nation has ever grown. But we have forgotten God."[50]

If we pull out a ten dollar bill, we see Alexander Hamilton, the first Secretary of the Treasury, under George Washington. Years earlier, he had attended the Constitutional Convention, and had this to say: "For my own part, I sincerely esteem [the Constitution] a system which without the finger of God, never could have been suggested and agreed upon by such a diversity of interests."[51]

If we pull out a $20 bill, we see Andrew Jackson, our seventh president. He said that the Bible is the "rock upon which our republic rests."[52]

On the $50 bill is the face of Ulysses S. Grant. Although he had a serious problem with drinking, even he apparently made his peace with God by the end of his life. He once declared of the Bible, "To the influence of this Book are we indebted for all the progress made in true civilization, and to this must we look as our guide in the future. 'Righteousness exalteth a nation; but sin is a reproach to any people.'"[53]

Finally, a $100 bill has the face of Benjamin Franklin, a man who apparently was not an orthodox Christian. Yet, even he saw the importance of Christianity in society. He did not believe it was wrong for public officials to pray. In fact, he encouraged it.

When he served on a committee in July 1776 to propose a seal for the newly born country, he suggested, "Moses lifting up his wand, and dividing the red sea, and pharaoh in his chariot overwhelmed with the waters. This motto: 'Rebellion to tyrants is obedience to God.'"[54]

WASHINGTON COULD SEE GOD AT WORK

We all know that Benedict Arnold committed treason. But George Washington happened to stumble on that information quite by accident. He attributed learning of it—in time before Arnold could inflict real and fatal damage on the American cause—to God. On that occasion, Washington sent the following letter to his troops, dated September 26, 1780:

> .... Happily the treason had been timely discovered to prevent the fatal misfortune. The providential train of circumstances which led to it affords the most convincing proof that the Liberties of America are the object of divine Protection.[55]

In 1778, George Washington wrote a letter to a fellow patriot, Thomas Nelson, Jr., in which he marveled at how much the Lord was helping the American cause, "The hand of Providence has been so conspicuous in all this [the colonies' victories in the American War for Independence], that he must be worse than an infidel that lacks faith, and more than wicked, that has not gratitude enough to acknowledge his obligations."[56]

In other words, God has helped us so much that anyone who can't see that and can't thank Him must be worse than an unbeliever.

Declaring independence from Great Britain was a slow train coming. It didn't happen overnight. The colonists tried virtually every remedy to keep the peace, but not at the expense of giving up their God-given liberties.

These liberties included religious liberty. Great Britain was threatening to impose the Church of England and its system of bishops on the colonies, once England had squashed the rebellion. This would mean that everything these dissident Protestants had accomplished in America—in all their settlements, charters, covenants, town halls, schools, colleges, and so on—would be undone.

THE FRENCH AND INDIAN WARS

In the 1750s, the French and Indian Wars took place in America. Great Britain joined forces with American colonists against the French, which desired more territory in what is now the United States. It was in this war that some Americans learned the art of warfare—especially George Washington. The French joined forces with the Indians.

England and America defeated the French and the Indians, but the cost was enormous. So in the 1760s, the king and Parliament wanted to recoup some of the losses by making the Americans help pay for the war now that it was over. It sounded reasonable; however, they didn't allow American input into their series of taxes imposed on the colonists to pay for the war. There was taxation but no representation. This violated the God-given rights of the colonists and was contrary to their rights as British subjects, even if an ocean separated them from the Motherland.

In the early 1770s, the tension was mounting in the colonies. King George III exacerbated the situation by appointing loyalist governors who were often tyrannical toward the American colonists. One of these appointed governors wrote a letter back to England that was read on the floor of the British Parliament, reflecting where Americans' loyalty lay: "If you ask an American, who is his master? He will tell you he has none, nor any governor but Jesus Christ."[57]

In the meantime, the founders of this nation made many attempts at peace. Even as late as the early 1770s, a free and independent America was virtually beyond imagination.

Meanwhile, the patriots proclaimed: "Nothing is more foreign from our hearts than a spirit of rebellion, notwithstanding we have been contending these ten years with Great Britain for our rights. What can they gain by the victory, should they subjugate us? What will be the glory of enslaving their children and brothers? Nay, how great will be the danger to their own liberties!"[58] In short, the sentiment among the early Americans was to work out their conflicts with the British, while maintaining their rights as British subjects. Since God was the source of these rights, they were non-negotiable. The colonists were not a rebellious people and could not see what benefit the British would gain by ruling over their own brothers.

But the British mistreatment of some of the colonies, Massachusetts in particular, was beginning to provoke other colonies. Before the war, George Washington once remarked to a British officer serving under General Thomas Gage: "The Massachusetts people are every day receiving fresh proofs of a systematic assertion of arbitrary power."[59] And he added, "It is not the wish of that government, or any other upon this continent, separately or collectively, to set up for independence; but none of them will ever submit to the loss of those rights and privileges without which life, liberty, and property are rendered totally insecure."[60]

THE PORT ACT

Schooled in a Christian view of government, the colonists believed their rights were given by God. But England was soon to test that conviction. In the 1760s and 1770s, the British Parliament, in cahoots with the king, passed a series of acts to unreasonably tax, subdue, and control the American colonists—again, to pay back some of their losses in the French and Indian War. One of the most vexing of these measures passed in Parliament was the Port Act (1774), which closed the harbor of that most rebellious American city, Boston—location of the Boston Tea Party in December 1773. What the British did not count on was that the other colonists would come to the aid of the Bostonians.

In fact, they actively tried to discourage other colonies from helping by publishing lies abroad in those colonies. Bancroft points out, "It was published at the corners of the streets that Pennsylvania would refuse to suspend commerce; that the Society of Friends [the Quakers] would arrest every step toward war; that New York would never name deputies to a congress; that the power of Great Britain could not fail to crush resistance."[61]

On June 1, 1774, at midnight, the Port Act went into effect, as scheduled. British ships converged into Boston Harbor to begin an indefinite blockade. George Bancroft describes the somber response from two other American colonies: "At Philadelphia, the bells of the churches were muffled and tolled, the ships in port hoisted their colors at half mast . . . In Virginia, the population thronged the churches; Washington attended the service and strictly kept the fast."[62] George Washington's diary entry for June 1, 1774 reads, "Went to church and fasted all day."[63]

Great Britain had thrown down the gauntlet. But if they thought they were picking a fight merely with Boston, they were badly mistaken.

All the colonies were moved to help Boston, or at least sympathize with it. It took only three weeks for the American colonies to make Boston's business their business. The Continental Congress reprimanded General Thomas Gage, the British military leader responsible for closing the harbor. They accused him of engaging in behavior tending "to involve a free people in the horrors of war."[64]

After Britain blockaded the Boston port, William Prescott of Pepperell, Massachusetts, encouraged the people of that city: "We heartily sympathize with you, and are always ready to do all in our power for your support, comfort and relief, knowing that Providence has placed you where you must stand the first shock. We consider that we are all embarked in (the same boat) and must sink or swim together. . . . Let us all be of one heart, and stand fast in the liberty wherewith Christ has made us free. And may He, of His infinite mercy, grant us deliverance of all our troubles."[65]

The people of Boston received more than moral support. Support from other colonies poured into Boston—generous donations of food and other needed supplies. South Carolina was the first to respond with two hundred barrels of rice. Throughout New England, towns sent grain, peas, oil, fish, livestock, and money to help the people of Boston. The people of Norfolk sent a very touching letter of support, "Our hearts are warmed with affection for you . . . we address the Almighty

Ruler to support you in your afflictions; be assured we consider you as suffering in the common cause, and look upon ourselves as bound by the most sacred ties to support you."[66]

The people of Boston and their fellow colonists up and down the American coast could have lain down and just submitted to all the abuse the British were heaping on them. But if they did, they would be forfeiting their liberty and their conviction that our rights are God-given. George Bancroft points out that the freedom-loving Americans could not do this:

> But a people who were trained to read and write; to discuss all political questions, privately and in public; to strive to exhibit in their lives the Christian system of ethics, the beauty of holiness, and the unselfish nature of virtue; to reason on the great ends of God in creation; to believe in their own immortality; and to venerate their ancestry as above all others pure, enlightened, and free—could never forego the civil rights which were their most cherished inheritance.[67]

To be fair, the king of England was not the only inflexible character in this drama. There were some unyielding colonists like Samuel Adams, who saw independence as inevitable and worth fighting for. Adams' deep commitment to his Christian faith emboldened him to make this stance. Many, in New England in particular, were not willing to consider compromise, for too much was at stake.

The British army and navy descended upon Boston, trying to force the city the Puritans had built into submission.

THE REGULATING ACT

One of the major bones of contention was the charter of Massachusetts. In the 1620s, King Charles I, no friend of the Puritans, had granted the original charter of Massachusetts. Later that charter came under attack under his Catholic son, James II, but the charter was finally re-secured by William and Mary. This charter let the Puritans be Puritans. It let them worship Jesus Christ in the way they saw fit, recognizing their God-given rights.

But in 1774, the British Parliament and king revoked the charter, jeopardizing the longstanding practice of the town hall meetings and placing the colony under capricious British rule. The guarantees for freedom, including religious freedom, were no longer in place. The Whig Party in Parliament greatly condemned this measure. But they were in the minority.

What the king was doing to Massachusetts, he had plans to do to Connecticut and Rhode Island. Add to that, England, as noted above, wanted to impose the Anglican Church (and their bishops) on the whole of America. Steven J. Keillor writes, "Dissenters feared that the Church of England would send an Anglican bishop to the colonies."[68] Thus, the whole Puritan "errand into the wilderness" was about to be extinguished. One-hundred-fifty years of freedom, earned at the expense of blood, sweat, and toil, could well have all been in vain.

George Bancroft writes, "[Lord] North was willing to restore the charter of Massachusetts; the king wished rather to renounce America."[69]

George Bancroft points out how serious this Regulating Act was:

> Without previous notice to Massachusetts and without a hearing, it took away rights and liberties which the people had enjoyed from the foundation of the colony, except in the evil days of James II, and which had been renewed in the charter from William and Mary. . . .[70]
> . . . This regulating act, moreover, uprooted the dearest institution of New England, whose people, from the first settlement of the country, had been accustomed in their town-meetings to transact all business that touched them most nearly as fathers, as freemen, and as Christians.[71]

What is the basis of our rights? Bancroft notes that Continental Congressman "[Richard Henry] Lee of Virginia rested them on nature. 'Our ancestors,' he said, 'found here no government, and, as a consequence, had a right to make their own. Charters are an unsafe reliance, for the king's right to grant them has itself been denied. Besides, the right to life and the right to liberty are inalienable.'"[72]

More and more colonists began to realize that the freedoms their forefathers sacrificed so much for was to be lost in this particular generation. After the charter of Massachusetts was revoked, American military leader William Prescott said:

> We think, if we submit to these regulations, all is gone. Our forefathers passed the vast Atlantic, spent their blood and treasure that they might enjoy their liberties, both civil and religious, and transmit them to their posterity. Their children have waded through seas of difficulty, to leave us free and happy in the enjoyment of English privileges. Now, if we should give them up, can our children rise up and call us blessed? Is a glorious death in defense of our liberties better than a short infamous life, and our memories to be had in detestation to the latest posterity?[73]

Similarly, the people of Middlesex met at Concord in 1774 and declared: "Our fathers left us a fair inheritance, purchased by blood and treasure; this we are resolved to transmit equally fair to our children; no danger shall affright, no difficulties intimidate us; and if, in support of our rights, we are called to encounter even death, we are yet undaunted; sensible that he can never die too soon who lays down his life in support of the laws and liberties of his country."[74]

The people of Massachusetts were grieved and angry with this revocation of their charter and with being subjected to arbitrary British control. Even loyalist General Thomas Gage wrote to the king and suggested this was too much for the colonists to bear, and that they had friends up and down the American coast. He suggested that this and other taxing measures be overturned. But the king was upset to hear these things, and he declared, "The New England governments are now in a state of rebellion; blows must decide whether they are to be subject to this country or to be independent."[75]

In turn, when Ben Franklin heard of the king's response, he told his closest associates that the only safety for America was as a free country. This reminds me of what William Lisle Bowles said to Edmund Burke, one of the few British statesmen to oppose the war against America: "The cause of freedom is the cause of God."[76]

Jefferson lists more than twenty specific complaints against the King of England in the Declaration of Independence. One of these alludes to this Regulating Act: "For taking away our charters, abolishing our most valuable laws, and altering fundamentally the forms of our governments."[77]

Correctly perceiving the times, Samuel Adams declared: "An empire is rising in America; and Britain, by her multiplied oppressions, is accelerating that independency which she dreads. We have a post to maintain, to desert which would entail upon us the curses of posterity. The virtue of our ancestors inspires us; they were contented with clams and mussels. For my own part, I have been wont to converse with poverty; and I can live happily with her the remainder of my days, if I can thereby contribute to the redemption of my country."[78] Sam Adams was willing to live in poverty, eating just "clams and mussels" as his Puritan forefathers had, as long as he could live in freedom.

AND YET—INDEPENDENCE WAS SLOW IN THE MAKING

To say that Americans woke up one day and decided to fight for their independence would be inaccurate. It was a long process for many of them to become convinced that war was the only option. For example, in 1775 in South Carolina, the colonists assured their new royalist governor that they had no wish for Independence and that their loyalty lay with the crown, but they also made it clear that death was to be preferred to slavery.

But the lines were being clearly drawn. Although Boston

was the hotbed of much opposition, the official control of the city was in the hands of the loyalists—so much so that the city itself became a refuge to the anti-American forces. George Bancroft writes, "Outside of Boston, the king's rule was at an end. The wealthy royalists, who entertained no doubt that all resistance would soon be crushed, were silent from fear, or fled to Boston as their 'only asylum.'"[79] This gives evidence that Boston was under British control.

It would remain that way until the brilliant rescue by General George Washington in 1776, who one night gained control of Dorchester Heights, allowing him to control much of the city of Boston. Washington managed to sneak large cannons up on the heights without British notice and oust the surprised British troops. After this strategic victory, the liberated men of the city declared to General Washington, "Next to the Divine Power, we ascribe to your wisdom that this acquisition has been made with so little effusion of human blood. . . ."[80]

ONE MORE PETITION TO THE KING

Despite all the British had done and were threatening to do, even as late as 1774, the Congress decided to petition the king again to try and work out a reconciliation. Congress assigned the petition-writing task to John Dickinson, who was from the portion of Pennsylvania that ultimately became the state of Delaware. Bancroft says of this petition that every line of it was imbued "with a desire for conciliation."[81] The petition declared "Your royal authority over us, and our connection with Great Britain, we shall always support and maintain."[82] They even appealed to the king as a type of father figure. They referred to him "as the loving father of his whole people," and sought "his interposition for their relief and a gracious answer to their petition."[83]

The specific issue at hand dealt with tax laws the King and Parliament had imposed on the colonists. The Americans were upset that they hadn't been consulted in the process—no taxation without representation. They viewed their liberty as a sacred gift of God, not to be arbitrarily taken away. Although the catalyst for the conflict could be said, superficially, to be "taxation without representation," there was a much deeper principle here. The British government was arbitrarily abusing power at the Americans' expense, and they felt that they must resist this abuse.

To cope with unfair taxes and tariffs, the colonists had to be resourceful. So, for example, they made their clothes at home. They would have preferred clothes from abroad to the crude homespun wardrobe, so they reasoned with the king in this petition that they were sacrificing comfort, but meanwhile Britain was losing money by the loss of exports to the Americans. Bancroft points out how the Americans virtually groveled before the king for a peaceful solution that wouldn't compromise their liberties.

Meanwhile, as Congress hopefully worked toward a peaceful solution, they also did something unique—they recognized the authority of the citizens. Bancroft writes "This first American congress brought forth another measure, which was without an example [precedent]. It recognized the political being and authority of the people."[84] Also John Adams requested "gunpowder and cash" for New England, which was feeling the brunt of British pressure. The truth of what James Otis had asserted earlier in "The Rights of the British Colonies Asserted and Proved" was beginning to be realized: "God Almighty . . . has given to all men a natural right to be free, and they have it ordinarily in their power to make themselves so, if they please."[85]

On October 8, 1775, the Second Continental Congress resolved "that this congress approved the opposition of the inhabitants of the Massachusetts Bay to the execution of the late acts of parliament, and, if the same shall be attempted to be carried into execution by force, all America ought to support them in their opposition."[86] This motion passed, but the vote was not unanimous. George Bancroft notes the effect of this vote on the king: "This is the vote which hardened George III to listen to no terms."[87]

ARROGANCE OF THE BRITISH

The arrogance against Americans on the part of many in the House of Lords can be seen in the sneer of the Earl of Sandwich: "Americans are neither disciplined nor capable of discipline; their numbers will only add to the facility of their defeat. . . ."[88] Furthermore, he made the House laugh with comical remarks about the colonists' cowardice. The British haughtily assumed they could easily crush the Americans. The French minister, Garnier, observed, "They have neither a marine, nor allies, nor a prince of Orange."[89] Meanwhile, loyalists in America shared the same contempt for the ragtag army that dared to take on the strongest army in the world. Bancroft writes, "On these bustling preparations of men who had no artillery, few muskets with bayonets, and no treasury, the loyalists looked with derision, never doubting the power of Great Britain to crush every movement of insurrection."[90]

George Washington believed that war should not be entered into lightly—only as the last resort. But when the need arises, he said: "That no man should scruple, or hesitate a moment to use arms in defense of so valuable a blessing as freedom, on which all the good and evil of life depends, is clearly my opinion; yet arms . . . should be the last resource."[91]

This arrogance on the part of the British can even be seen in the early skirmishes of the war. For example, at the Battle of Bunker Hill, the veteran British troops expected to easily take the field. They eventually did, but this was, at best, a Pyrrhic victory, the kind where the victor's losses are so great, it could hardly be viewed as a victory.

George Bancroft points out:

> American independence was not an act of sudden passion, nor the work of one man or one assembly. It had been discussed in every part of the country by farmers and merchants, by mechanics and planters, by the fishermen and the backwoodsmen; in town-meetings and from the pulpit; at social gatherings and around the camp fires; in newspapers and in pamphlets; in county conventions and conference of

committees; in colonial congresses and assemblies.[92]

Some of the British soldiers who mocked the Americans before the war as cowards who would flee at the first shot, now found their lives spared only by, in the words of Bancroft, "the rapidity of their retreat."[93]

The British General in charge of Massachusetts, Thomas Gage, was recalled to England after the fiasco of Bunker Hill. But before that time, while he still had his job, he warned England: "The conquest of this country is not easy; you have to cope with vast numbers. In all their wars against the French, they never showed so much conduct, attention, and perseverance as they do now. I think it my duty to let your lordship know the true situation of affairs."[94]

WILLIAM PITT

William Pitt, who later became the Earl of Chatham, was the great orator in the House of Commons. He provided a voice for opposition among Britons against the attempt to squash American liberty. He championed the cause of American freedom in Parliament. The problem was that physical illness prevented him from playing a greater role in opposing the king, the monarch's cabinet, and the opponents of American liberty in the House of Commons and the House of Lords. Pitt, for whom the city of Pittsburgh was named, was a great admirer of the Continental Congress.

Pitt warned his fellow countrymen that they would regret their actions against American independence: "The histories of Greece and Rome give us nothing equal to it [the congress at Philadelphia], and all attempts to impose servitude upon such a mighty continental nation must be vain. We shall be forced ultimately to retract; let us retract while we can, not when we must."[95]

BEN FRANKLIN

The able statesman Ben Franklin spent considerable time trying to work out an honorable solution to both sides in the conflict. He traveled to Britain and witnessed proceedings at Parliament in 1774, wherein he realized that a peaceful, honorable compromise was becoming increasingly impossible. He was warned by some British of the consequences of American obstinacy. He answered "My liberty property... consists of houses in those towns; make bonfires of them whenever you please; the fear of losing them will never alter my resolution to resist to the last the claim of parliament."[96] He told his fellow Americans: "The eyes of all Christendom are now upon us, and our honor as a people is become a matter of the utmost consequence. If we tamely give up our rights in this contest, a century to come will not restore us in the opinion of the world; we shall be stamped with the character of dastards, poltroons, and fools; and be despised and trampled upon, not by this haughty, insolent nation only, but by all mankind. Present inconveniences are therefore to be borne with fortitude, and better times expected."[97] Later he told his British friends in a letter "Americans will fight; England has lost her colonies forever."[98]

NEW YORK AND ALEXANDER HAMILTON

Meanwhile, opposition to rebellion on the part of some Americans appeared to be based on expedient measures. They thought that England, the most powerful nation on earth, could decimate the colonies if they chose. In February 1775, the New York assembly voted 17-9 to not send delegates to the next Continental Congress. The nine dissenters made a strong case for American independence, but not strong enough, for their opponents declared:

> But Great Britain will enforce her claims by fire and sword. The Americans are without fortresses, without disciplines, without military stores, without money, and cannot keep an army in the field; nor can troops be disciplined without regular pay and government by an unquestioned legal authority. A large number of armed men might be got together near Boston, but in a week they would be obliged to

disperse to avoid starving.[99]

Thus, the facts of immense British superiority were not lost on some of the colonists.

However, one New Yorker began to emerge as a strong voice for American independence. Alexander Hamilton, a Dutch Reformed native of the Caribbean islands, chose to leave his homeland after a devastating hurricane. Studying at Columbia College in New York, Hamilton became a champion for the American cause. He argued, "The Supreme Intelligence who rules the world has constituted an eternal law, which is obligatory upon all mankind, prior to any human institution whatever. He gave existence to man, together with the means of preserving and beautifying that existence; and invested him with an inviolable right to pursue liberty and personal safety. Natural liberty is a gift of the Creator to the whole human race. Civil liberty is only natural liberty, modified and secured by the sanctions of civil society. It is not dependent on human caprice; but it is conformable to the constitution of man, as well as necessary to the well-being of society."[100]

Hamilton was an important founding father, and though not always faithful in his Christian walk, he certainly believed in Jesus Christ. He once remarked, "I have carefully examined the evidences of the Christian religion, and if I was sitting as a juror upon its authenticity I would unhesitatingly give my verdict in its favor. I can prove its truth as clearly as any proposition ever submitted to the mind of man."[101]

Hamilton made a strong case that our rights are God-given: "The sacred rights of mankind are not to be rummaged for among old parchments or musty records. They are written, as with a sunbeam, in the whole volume of human nature, by the hand of the divinity itself; and can never be erased or obscured by mortal power."[102]

A DAY OF FASTING

Americans took great pains to try and avoid the war, but British arrogance mitigated against it. Attempt after attempt to reconcile failed. Then, a few months after the attack on Lexington and Concord (April 19, 1775), Congress asked the people to fast and pray for peace. George Bancroft writes: "On the twelfth of June [1775] the general congress made its first appeal to the people of the twelve united colonies by enjoining them to keep a fast on one and the same day, on which they were to recognize 'King George III as their rightful sovereign, and to look up to the great Governor of the world for the restoration of the invaded rights of America and a reconciliation with the parent state.'"[103]

Any hopes for reconciliation, however, were fading when Congress declared in 1775: "We have counted the cost of this contest, and find nothing so dreadful as voluntary slavery. Our cause is just, our union is perfect, our internal resources are great, and, if necessary, foreign assistance is undoubtedly attainable. Before God and the world, we declare that the arms we have been compelled by our enemies to assume we will employ for the preservation of our liberties; being, with one mind, resolved to die free men rather than live slaves. We have not raised armies with designs of separating from Great Britain and establishing independent states. Necessity has not yet driven us into that desperate measure."[104]

But it soon would.

And so George Washington would declare, "Unhappy it is to reflect that a brother's sword has been sheathed in a brother's breast, and that the once happy and peaceful plains of America are either to be drenched with blood or inhabited by slaves. Sad alternative! But can a virtuous man hesitate in his choice?"[105]

But God was at work in all this. And the United States of America would be the result.

CONCLUSION

With perfect hindsight, it's easy to see how God had His hand in the founding of our nation. The Americans did their best to keep peace, but the king's obstinacy led to what seemed to be an inevitable break with the colonies.

One of the greatest hymns ever produced in America was written by James Russell Lowell in 1849; it talks about God at work behind the scenes. When Dr. Martin Luther King finally made it to Selma (after all the dogs, police brutality, and water cannons), he read the words from this classic hymn by Lowell:

> Once to every man and nation, comes the moment to decide, In the strife of truth with falsehood, for the good or evil side; Some great cause, some great decision, offering each the bloom or blight, And the choice goes by forever, 'twixt that darkness and that light.
>
> Then to side with truth is noble, when we share her wretched crust, [Before] her cause bring fame and profit, and 'tis prosperous to be just; Then it is the brave man chooses while the coward stands aside, Till the multitude make virtue of the faith they had denied.
>
> ....
>
> Though the cause of evil prosper, yet the truth alone is strong; Though her portion be the scaffold, and upon the throne be wrong; Yet that scaffold sways the future, and behind the dim unknown, Standeth God within the shadow, keeping watch above His own.[106]

Although the American colonists faithfully persevered to try to prevent war, God "behind the dim unknown" was "keeping watch above his own." And our nation was born. A nation which has given so much freedom to so many—when we have followed God's principles. The Gospel has gone out from America's shores like never before. But as we move away from God, we're losing all this.

May God grant us the grace that more and more Americans repent, accept the Gospel, and live it out. The impact could be enormous, producing eternal fruit.

CHAPTER THREE

Education

The only foundation for a useful education
in a republic is to be laid in RELIGION....
Without this, there can be no virtue, and without
virtue there can be no liberty, and liberty is the
object and life of all republican governments. . . .
the religion I mean to recommend in this place
is the religion of JESUS CHRIST.[107]

Declaration Signer
Benjamin Rush

Founding father Benjamin Rush noted this about the Bible and the schools: "...this divine book, above all others, favors that equality among mankind, that respect for just laws, and all those sober and frugal virtues which constitute the soul of republicanism." When and if schools ignore teaching the Bible, "I lament that we waste so much time and money in punishing crimes and take so little pains to prevent them."[108]

Education was important to the founding fathers. It's important to us. As James Madison said, "A well-instructed people alone can be permanently a free people."[109]

In his Farewell Address in 1796, George Washington noted, "Promote...as an object of primary importance institutions for the general diffusion of knowledge."[110]

Patrick Henry noted how it is good for society that children learn Christianity:

> The general diffusion of Christian knowledge hath a natural tendency to correct the morals of men, restrain their vices, and preserve the peace of society. . . .[111]

John Adams pointed out that schools should not be loose in their teaching of morals: "In vain are Schools, Academies, and Universities instituted, if loose Principles and licentious habits are impressed upon Children in their earliest years. . . .[112]

EDUCATION AT THE LOWER LEVEL

The American founders, even the handful of ones with questionable religious opinions, had a biblical worldview. They were taught the Bible virtually all their lives. They even learned their ABCs from biblical truths.

For example, millions of copies of the *New England Primer* were reproduced from 1692 until about 1900 and were used to teach Americans how to read and write. This book also taught them about the Bible. Here is what the primer said on the ABCs. Think about this: Samuel Adams, John Adams, John Hancock, Paul Revere, Ben Franklin, and so on, learned their

ABCs through the prism of biblical truths:

A
In ADAM'S
Fall
We sinned all.

B
Heaven to find;
The Bible
Mind.

C
Christ crucify'd
For sinners
dy'd.

D
The Deluge
drown'd
The Earth
around.

E
ELIJAH hid
By Ravens fed.

F
The judgment
made
 FELIX afraid.

G
As runs the
Glass,
Our Life doth
pass.

H
My Book and
Heart
Must never
part.

I [sic]
JOB feels the
Rod,—
Yet blesses
GOD.

K
Proud Korah's
troop
Was swallowed
up

L
LOT fled to
Zoar,
Saw fiery
Shower
On Sodom
pour.

M
MOSES was he
Who Israel's
Host
Led thro' the
Sea

N
NOAH did
view
The old world
& new.

O
Young
OBADIAS,
DAVID,
JOSIAS,
All were pious.

P
PETER deny'd
His Lord and
cry'd.

Q
Queen
ESTHER sues
And saves the
Jews.

R
Young pious
RUTH,
Left all for
Truth.

S
Young SAM'L
dear,
The Lord did
fear.

T
Young
TIMOTHY
Learnt sin to
fly.

U [sic]
VASHTI for
Pride
Was set aside.

W
Whales in the
Sea,
GOD's Voice
obey.

X
XERXES did
die,
And so must I.

Y
While youth do
chear
Death may be
near.

Z
ZACCHEUS he
Did climb the
Tree
Our Lord to
see.[113]

So the colonial children of America, including many of our founding fathers, not only learned their ABCs at school; they also learned important truths from the Bible at the same time.

This *New England Primer* even included the Lord's Prayer, the Apostles' Creed, and the shorter catechism of the Westminster Confession of Faith (with its 100-plus questions and answers about God). A colonial student who knew his primer well was better acquainted with the historic Christian faith than are the vast majority of active church-goers in modern America. The primer was used not only in New England, but beyond as well.

Many of our founding fathers were weaned on biblical truth. Even those who weren't taught from this primer were taught the Scriptures in school.

Rick Green, who works with David Barton to help promote America's true history, once said this about the founders and the Bible: "Well, I think it would be an understatement to say that the founding fathers were knowledgeable about the Bible. I think their knowledge of the Bible, compared to ours, today, even those that would say: you know, I'm a Christian, I read the Bible daily; I live out my religious faith. We are extremely inadequate in our understanding of biblical principles—in our worldview, compared to the founding fathers."[114]

EDUCATION AT THE HIGHER LEVEL

Dr. Donald Lutz of the University of Houston said this about the knowledge of the Bible and our founders: "Yale trained ministers, Harvard trained ministers, and so they spent their time, effectively, in a kind of a pre-minister curriculum. And certainly, [the founders] learned the Bible—they learned it down to their fingertips."[115]

We forget sometimes about the deeply Christian origins of all of America's first colleges, including Harvard, which was founded to train ministers of the Gospel of Jesus Christ. Even today, you can see written in stone (in old English) these words at one of the school's entrances:

After God had carried us safe to New England,

and we had built our houses, provided necessities for our livelihood, reared convenient places for God's worship, and settled the civil government; one of the next things we longed for, and looked after was to advance learning, and perpetuate it to posterity; dreading to leave an illiterate ministry to the churches, when our present ministers shall lie in the dust.[116]

This is not too subtle. Is it?

All the original colleges and universities—all of them (certainly as early as the founding era)—were thoroughly Christian. They were founded by the sweat and blood of Christians for Christian purposes. This includes Harvard, Yale, Princeton, Brown, Dartmouth, and Columbia. Many of these schools today stand for the exact opposite. But the liberals didn't start these schools. They just eventually took them over, turning them away from God.

Consider just a quick run-down of these schools that many of our founders attended:

- The original motto of Harvard was (in Latin): Truth for Christ and the Church. In the early 20th century, they jettisoned everything after the word Veritas (Truth). Founded in 1630, named after Rev. John Harvard, a 1643 statement of the school's goals said, "Every one shall consider the main End of his life and studies, to know God and Jesus Christ which is Eternal life. John 17:3."[117]

- William and Mary was Anglican in its founding and as such, Jesus Christ was pre-eminent. Among other things, two of the Statutes of the College of William and Mary (1727) state the school's purpose: "That the Churches of America, especially Virginia, should be supplied with good Ministers after the Doctrine and Government of the Church of England; and that the College should be a constant

Seminary for this Purpose... That the Indians of America should be instructed in the Christian Religion...."[118]

- Yale was founded to train ministers of the Gospel in the Connecticut area in 1700, and named after the Puritan benefactor, Elihu Yale. Its 1745 charter stated, "All scholars shall live religious, godly, and blameless lives according to the rules of God's Word, diligently reading the Holy Scriptures, the fountain of light and truth; and constantly attend upon all the duties of religion, both in public and secret."[119]

- An early advertisement for King's College, which opened in 1754 and is now Columbia University, read: "The chief thing that is aimed at in this college is to teach and engage children to know God in Jesus Christ."[120]

- Rev. Jonathan Dickinson was the first president of the College of New Jersey, which later became known as Princeton. Dickinson once said, "Cursed be all that learning that is contrary to the cross of Christ."[121] Its official motto even now is reported to be, "Under God's Power She Flourishes."[122]

- Dartmouth was originally founded for the purpose of training ministers of the Gospel and missionaries to the Indians.

And on and on it goes. Too bad we have been cut off from this important tradition.

Furthermore, David Barton, author and speaker on America's Christian heritage, points out that about half (27, at last count) of the signers (56 men) of the Declaration of Independence had the equivalent of seminary degrees.

THE NORTHWEST ORDINANCE

The first Congress under the new Constitution gave us the First Amendment and also passed a law that ensured that each state and territory to be added to the new nation would also be committed to building schools. If the American experiment were to work, it could only do so if the people could read and write for themselves. So on August 4, 1789, Congress passed the Northwest Ordinance (a provision they had also passed a few years earlier when the Articles of Confederation rather than the Constitution was the law of the land. They called it the "Northwest Ordinance" in reference to expanding territory north and west beyond the Appalachians—initially, the area west of the original colonies, but east of the Mississippi. This included what is now Ohio, Illinois, Indiana, etc. But the Northwest Ordinance, as one of our founding documents, was extended to all new territory and states of the United States.

And what does the Northwest Ordinance stipulate? This is most instructive. Would that modern educators read this act passed by the very same Congress that gave us the First Amendment:

> Religion, morality and knowledge being essential to good government and the happiness of mankind, schools and the means of education shall forever be encouraged.[123]

The Northwest Ordinance shows us what the founders intended—that education and religion and morality went hand-in-hand. But this is the opposite of what we see happening today.

God has been thrown out of the schools. The kids have gotten dumber, and many of the schools have become unsafe.

"DON'T KNOW MUCH ABOUT HISTORY"

George Orwell wrote in his classic novel, *1984*: "Who controls the past, controls the future: who controls the present controls the past."[124]

So there's a battle over history. That battle continues in our day.

A recent survey finds that many of our young people are failing to learn basic facts of our history. For example, only 35% of fourth-graders know the purpose of the Declaration of

Independence.

That's scary because if we don't know where we came from, we don't know where we are going. That's a paraphrase of President Woodrow Wilson.

Our 28th president said in a rally speech in 1911 before his election: "A nation which does not remember what it was yesterday, does not know what it is today, nor what it is trying to do. We are trying to do a futile thing if we do not know where we came from or what we have been about...."[125] He went on to speak of our Christian heritage.

A report from the National Assessment of Educational Progress in 2010 found there has been little overall educational progress since 2006. The survey found that only 20% of fourth graders in this country and only 17% of eighth graders were in the category of "proficient" or "advanced." That means 80% or more were not proficient. They found that more than half of all high school seniors showed a less-than-basic knowledge about our history.

It's true what the old song says: "Don't know much about history." At one time, America was one of the best educated nations in the world. In New England, after generations of Puritan influence, John Adams remarked that finding an illiterate man in New England was as rare as a comet. The founders understood that our experiment in self-government could only be maintained by a well-educated populace. That's why an accurate grasp of history matters.

PRAYER IN THE SCHOOLS

In America, the school day began in prayer for the first three hundred years of our experience. And, no, the First Amendment wasn't under assault because of it. But there has been a gradual assault on common sense and common courtesy since school prayer has been banned. God has been kicked out of schools, and in His place have come the metal detectors.

One of the three critical Supreme Court decisions on prayer centered around then-14-year-old William J. Murray in the Baltimore Public Schools. His mother, Madalyn Murray

O'Hare, was for years the nation's leading atheist. Bill told me that in the early 1960s, his mother, who was divorced, tried to emigrate with her children into the Soviet Union. She had thought the atheists had ushered in the millennium, if you will, in the workers' paradise. But the Soviet officials in Russia told her to return home, that she could do more good for the cause back home.

She was very upset by this turn of events, and when she came home, the school year had already started. As she was bringing William in late for school one day in a Baltimore public school, she was angry to see and hear the school children reciting the Lord's Prayer. "What the &*&%$^&$ is this?" she asked. She sued, with Bill as the chief plaintiff, and won.

Today, all these years later, William J. Murray, around whom that pivotal case revolved, is an evangelical minister. He totally disagrees now with what he and his mother did then. Today he favors school prayer. I interviewed him for Christian television, and he said, "I would like people to take a look at the Baltimore public schools today versus what they were when I went to those schools in 1963 and my mother took prayer out of the schools. We didn't have armed guards in the hallways then when we had God in the classroom. But I'll guarantee you there are armed guards. In fact, the city school system of Baltimore now has its own armed police force."[126]

CONCLUSION

Founding father Benjamin Rush said of the Bible, "This divine book, above all others, favors that equality among mankind, that respect for just laws, and all those sober and frugal virtues which constitute the soul of republicanism."

Rush warned that if we stopped teaching the Bible in schools, we'd have to spend more time and money punishing the crime that resulted. We see virtually every day the fulfillment of his prediction.

I once interviewed bestselling author Ann Coulter. She made this observation about our schools today:

What the government schools do—it is the left's madrassas, and they propagandize to the children, six hours a day, 12 years of the child's life. I would give them the presidency, the House, the Senate, if we could have children for six hours a day to give them our religion. But no, no, that used to be the purpose of school, oddly enough, to teach biblical truths. No, that is absolutely prohibited. Now, it is baptism, it's six hours a day being brainwashed into the liberal religion. When, you know, you wonder why it takes kids until their age 30 to become [conservatives], (laughs). Well, they've just had 12 years in the government schools, then the universities. I mean, the ones who come crawling, scraping through all of that nonsense. Obviously, we're getting the smarter kids.[127]

We can truly lose our freedom if the vast majority of Americans become ignorant. Ben Franklin once said, "A nation of well informed men who have been taught to know and prize the rights which God has given them cannot be enslaved. It is in the region of ignorance that tyranny begins."[128]

What will it take to preserve our freedoms? It will take an educated and well-studied population. Can we gain back some of the educational ground we have lost?

Yes, we can, through Christian schools and home schooling. Many people have awakened to the sorry state of our public schools today. We are intensely grateful for any active Christians in the public schools who are serving as teachers or principals or assistants in any way. But tragically, too many of the schools have become religion-free zones (in reality, Christian-free zones).

There is an incredible irony in all this. Education for the masses was a Christian invention to help make sure that the Protestant Reformation would take hold. To teach the Bible was the reason schools for the masses were started in the first place. Meanwhile, today, in many urban settings, Catholic schools are a way out for children stuck with very poor alternatives.

Christian education is a lifeline to millions of children.

A key answer from the founding fathers for today is that we need vast educational reform and either a serious overhaul of many of our colleges and universities, or new ones all together. We are again in need of "Truth for Christ and His Church."

CHAPTER FOUR

Religious Liberty

If I could have entertained the slightest apprehension that the Constitution framed by the Convention, where I had the honor to preside, might possibly endanger the religious rights of any ecclesiastical Society, certainly I would never have placed my signature to it.[129]

George Washington

America was founded for religious liberty, but in our day that freedom is greatly under fire. Yet George Washington said that he would not even have signed the Constitution if he had known that someone would twist it to exclude religious freedom.

Rev. John Witherspoon noted that if religious liberty would go, so also would other liberties and vice versa. Said he, "There is not a single instance in history, in which civil liberty was lost, and religious liberty preserved entire. . . . If therefore we yield up our temporal property, we at the same time deliver the conscience into bondage. . . . [Governments are to] defend and secure rights of conscience in the most equal and impartial manner. . . ."[130]

Founding father Samuel Chase was one of the Maryland signers of the Declaration of Independence. He served as a U.S. Supreme Court Justice, 1796-1811. In a 1799 case, *Runkel v. Winemiller,* Justice Chase wrote the majority opinion:

> Religion is of general and public concern, and on its support depend, in great measure, the peace and good order of government, the safety and happiness of the people.
>
> By our form of government, the Christian religion is the established religion; and all sects and denominations of Christians are placed upon the same equal footing and are equally entitled to protection in their religious liberty.[131]

This so clearly flies in the face of the kind of misinformed opinions we hear today.

George Mason introduced a declaration of rights in the Virginia legislature. These rights included religious toleration. Historian George Bancroft notes, "Mason had written that all should enjoy the fullest toleration in the exercise of religion."[132] James Madison didn't like the word toleration because it implied an already established religion. Madison stated: "All men are equally entitled to the free exercise of religion, according to the dictates of conscience."[133]

It's instructive that the First Amendment lists our freedoms, the first being religious freedom. After that, comes freedom of speech. When FDR spoke about the four freedoms, the first one he listed was freedom of speech "and expression." The second was "freedom of every person to worship God in his own way everywhere in the world."[134] No, President Roosevelt, with all due respect, the first freedom our founders gave us was freedom of religion. It is from that freedom that all other freedoms flow.

To paraphrase Thomas Jefferson: Jesus Christ is the model of our liberties; He gave us a choice, even though He could have imposed His way on us. Jefferson here calls Jesus "the holy author of our religion":

> Almighty God hath created the mind free...all attempts to influence it by temporal punishments... are a departure from the plan of the holy author of our religion, who being lord both of body and mind, yet choose not to propagate it by coercions on either, as was in his Almighty power to do, but to exalt it by its influence on reason alone...[135]

I brought this passage up on a controversial panel on TV recently, and without even looking it up (it's found in the Virginia Bill for Religious Liberty, 1786), they dismissed out of hand—without a scintilla of evidence—that Jefferson was speaking about Jesus. The "holy author of our religion"? There's no one else he or his hearers could have had in mind other than Christ.

Ironically, as we shall see, a different passage from Jefferson has been so twisted and misused today as to deny our rights, especially our religious rights.

"SEPARATION OF CHURCH AND STATE"

Today, if you talk about America's true history—that is, our nation's rich godly heritage—then all of a sudden, you are supposedly violating the "separation of church and state," words not found in our Constitution. The founders clearly did not want one Christian denomination to lord it over the others—there would be no national denomination in America. Thank the Lord for that. As a Presbyterian, I wouldn't want the Anglicans (Episcopalians), and the Anglicans wouldn't want a Presbyterian-run government either.

What modern secularists advocate for today, though, is not really the separation of church and state so much as the separation of God and state. The vision of the ACLU, if they had their way, is honestly much closer to the vision of the failed Soviet Union, with its state-sanctioned atheism, than it is to the vision of the founders of the U.S. Even the less orthodox amongst our founders would come off like card-carrying members of the Christian Coalition by today's standards.

AN EXAMPLE OF OUR INCREASING SECULARISM

Recently, our nation honored the dead in commemorating the 10th anniversary of 9/11. Regardless of his political views, I was pleased that the President read Scripture (from Psalm 46).

But I was displeased that the mayor of New York City chose to not invite any Christian clergyman to participate, as this would supposedly violate the separation of church and state.

Thomas Jefferson is the author of the phrase "separation of church and state," as quoted by the Supreme Court. Of course, Jefferson was in France when the Constitution was written, nor did he directly participate in the writing of the Bill of Rights.

When Jefferson was president, he regularly attended divine services that were held in the largest Protestant church in Washington, D.C., at the time. Where were they held? In the chambers of the U.S. Capitol—before it was even completed.

The Establishment Clause of the First Amendment (the first of the Bill of Rights) has been construed to mean a strict wall of separation of church and state. But that's only been the interpretation for the last half century or so.

Earlier, "Congress shall make no law respecting an establishment of religion..." (the Establishment Clause) was understood to mean that the founders wanted no national denomination lording it over the others.

The Anglican Church, for instance, was the official state religion of Virginia, from 1607 until 1786, "by law established." Meanwhile, the founders—by their words and by their actions—showed over and over again that they intended religion (by which they meant Christianity in its various stripes) to flourish, even in the public arena, on a voluntary basis.

They also said in the First Amendment, "Congress shall make no law...prohibiting the free exercise [of religion]..." Technically, if the ACLU's interpretation of the Establishment Clause is right, what in the world is the president doing reading from the Holy Bible at an official function, no less?

ACKNOWLEDGING GOD IS NOT ESTABLISHING RELIGION

One of my heroes is the Hon. Roy S. Moore, the former Chief Justice of the Alabama Supreme Court. He got in trouble because of his Ten Commandments monument, which he refused to remove from the rotunda of the state judiciary building.

In fact, he lost his job by refusing to obey the order to remove the monument. I have had the privilege of interviewing Roy Moore starting in1995, when he first began to come to national attention. At that time, he was a circuit court judge in a small courtroom in Gadsden, Alabama. He had a hand-carved plaque of the Ten Commandments.

When he first put it up in his courtroom, he asked his wife Kayla if she thought it would be okay. She didn't think there would be a problem. He then said, "But what if somebody complained about it?"

He put it up and for years it went unnoticed.

Enter the ACLU.

When they learned about it, they took him to court over the issue. Although he lost initially, he was able to keep the Ten Commandments up, while on appeal.

Later, he ran for chief justice of the Alabama Supreme Court. Known as the Ten Commandments judge, he won handily.

After hours, so as not to disturb the workflow, he had the large monument installed in the rotunda of the building. This was about a month before 9/11. I was there with a TV crew from Coral Ridge Ministries (now Truth in Action Ministries).

The Ten Commandments monument had the Decalogue on the top of the cube. On the sides were many great quotes from our founding fathers.

Unfortunately, the ACLU, Americans United for the Separation of Church and State, and the Southern Poverty Law Center—all the usual suspects—sued Chief Justice Moore for violating the separation of church and state.

In all the interviews I did with Chief Justice Moore (which number about half a dozen, at least), he kept making one point very clear—over and over. Acknowledging God is not the same thing as establishing religion. The founders opposed establishing religion at the federal level, but they encouraged (and engaged in) the acknowledgement of God, even in public settings and places.

Even if you look at many of the monuments around Washington, D.C., many of which date to the 1930s, we find references to God all over the place. That is even true at the Supreme Court itself—an institution that has helped cut us off from our Christian past more than any other organ of government.

Roy Moore told our viewers in one interview:

> Of course, they're accusing me of the establishment of a religion, but that is not a religion. God is not a religion. Our Forefathers knew this very well, but we don't have to go back to the 1700s. We can look back to 1954, when the United States Congress, in putting "under God" in the Pledge, said very plainly, "It should be pointed out that the adoption of this legislation in no way runs contrary to the provisions of the First Amendment to the United States Constitution. This is not an act establishing a religion or one interfering with the free exercise of religion." And then they said this, something we've

forgotten, "A distinction must be made between the existence of religion as an institution and a belief in the sovereignty of God." You see, we don't make that distinction between religion and God anymore.[136]

In other words, acknowledging God is perfectly permissible—even in a public setting. But establishing a particular religion on the part of the federal government—that is what is prohibited. Here we are at a place where we have banished God from the public arena and we're suffering the consequences.

WHO'S RIGHT?

So who's right: Chief Justice Moore or the ACLU? Any honest look at the record would show that Chief Justice Moore is correct.

Just consider a few facts about the founding fathers and religion (or the acknowledgment of God). The very same men who wrote the First Amendment (words which are now being used to keep God, and certainly Jesus, out of the public arena) did the following:

- Created the system of chaplains for the military and for the legislature.
- Called for national days of fasting and prayer and thanksgiving.
- Adopted the Northwest Ordinance, which said that schools should be encouraged in America so that they could teach "Religion, morality, and knowledge" (in that order).
- Acknowledged the Christian Sabbath in the Constitution. Article 1, Section 7 includes this statement: "If any Bill shall not be returned by the President within ten Days (Sundays excepted)...."
- Said that God is the source of our rights (in the Declaration of Independence).
- Had presidents sworn in on the Holy Bible from the very beginning, adding the oath, "So

help me God" in the process.

- Delivered speeches that mentioned God over and over. (Included in this are a myriad of private letters that mention God, the Church, the Bible, etc. As an example, Dr. Peter Lillback and I have an Appendix in our tome, *George Washington's Sacred Fire,* which shows Washington's familiarity with the Bible. Over and over, phrases and words that come right from the pages of Scripture are to be found in his writings—both public and private).

The ACLU has done so much to cut us off from our true past through their lawsuits to remove any vestige of our Christian heritage from the public realm. I once interviewed the ACLU's then-executive director, Ira Glasser, for a documentary exposing the work of that radical organization. I asked him about the chaplains hired at taxpayers' expense. His response was illuminating. He said, "The fact that the rights that they established were violated after they were written is true about any right [they passed]."[137] So, in other words, what the founders intended, they just weren't able to hold to themselves. Or, looked at differently, we in modern times know better what this law means than those who actually passed it.

RELIGION IS NOT MERE ACKNOWLEDGMENT OF GOD

James Madison, one of the founders most influential in the writing of the U.S. Constitution, wrote a document in 1785, "Memorial and Remonstrance." Frankly, I first learned about it through my interviews with Roy Moore.

Madison defined what "religion" meant, and it certainly meant more than "acknowledging God." Madison wrote, "We hold it for a fundamental and undeniable truth, 'that religion or the duty which we owe to our Creator and the manner of discharging it, can be directed only by reason and conviction, not by force or violence."[138]

Madison went on to say that as Christians (and clearly by implication he counts himself in that number), we must recognize that not everyone shares our religious convictions. That's between them and God. It is not up to us or the state to interfere with their consciences. We will all give an account to God; it's not the state's job to enforce religious conformity. Here is Madison saying these things in his own words:

> Whilst we assert for ourselves a freedom to embrace, to profess and to observe the Religion which we believe to be of divine origin, we cannot deny an equal freedom to those whose minds have not yet yielded to the evidence which has convinced us. If this freedom be abused, it is an offence against God, not against man: To God, therefore, not to man, must an account of it be rendered.[139]

SEPARATION OF GOD AND STATE

In modern America, we not only separate the institution of the Church from the institution of the State, but we separate God from the State. If the latter were appropriate, then it's time to take a bulldozer to some of our national monuments in Washington, D.C., because many of them quote Scripture or refer to God.

If it were true that God should be totally separated from the state, then it's time to take a jackhammer to Abraham Lincoln's speeches engraved in bold letters in the Lincoln Memorial. Why? Some of his sentences are quotes from Scripture. For example, his second Inaugural Address is carved there, containing such sentences as: "Woe unto the world because of offenses; for it must needs be that offenses come, but woe to that man by whom the offense cometh" [Matthew 18:7] and "the judgments of the Lord are true and righteous altogether" [Psalm 19:9].

If God were to be separate from the state, then why does our money say, "In God We Trust"? Why do we have military and congressional chaplains? Why is the president sworn in with his hand on the Bible? We've been misled in the last several decades as to what the First Amendment is all about.

As we have seen repeatedly, the founders expected

religion—Christianity—to flourish on a voluntary basis.

OBSERVATIONS OF A FRENCHMAN

Alexis de Tocqueville was a Frenchman who visited America in the early 1830s. He noted that in his native France, religion and liberty were supposed enemies, whereas in America, he found them to be friends. In his classic book, *Democracy in America,* he wrote:

> There is no country in the whole world in which the Christian religion retains a greater influence over the souls of men than in America and there can be no greater proof of its utility, and of its conformity to human nature, than that its influence is most powerfully felt over the most enlightened and free nation on earth.[140]

THE *TRINITY* DECISION AND BEYOND

In 1892, the U.S. Supreme Court delivered the *Trinity* decision, wherein they declared "this is a Christian nation." They came to this conclusion after poring through all the documentary evidence. They studied all the charters, covenants, and early documents of America through the founding era and even beyond. The Supreme Court stated:

> This is a religious people. This is historically true. From the discovery of this continent to the present hour, there is a single voice making this affirmation ... these are not individual sayings, declarations of private persons: they are organic utterances; they speak the voice of the entire people ... these and many other matters which might be noticed, add a volume of unofficial declarations to the mass of organic utterances that this is a Christian nation.[141]

Writing in *The Washington Times,* writer Larry Witham points out how the *Trinity* decision was not alone in this type of conclusion:

In 1931 the U.S. Supreme Court noted that the United States is a Christian nation. In a mid-Atlantic summit with British Prime Minister Winston Churchill in the darkest hours of World War II, President Roosevelt who had described the United States as "the lasting concord between men and nations, founded on the principles of Christianity" asked the crew of an American warship to join him in a rousing chorus of the hymn "Onward Christian Soldiers."

In 1947, writing to Pope Pius XII, President Truman said flatly, "This is a Christian nation."

Nobody argued with any of them.[142]

I believe that groups like the ACLU that continually sue to remove any vestige of Christianity in public places are trying to remake America in the image of the failed Soviet Union, with its godless foundation. The founders did not intend a national denomination. But that's far different from what today's secularists are trying to impose with their myriad lawsuits—essentially, state-sanctioned atheism.

WHAT DID THE FOUNDERS INTEND BY THE FIRST AMENDMENT?

What then did the Founders intend with the "Establishment Clause" of the First Amendment—"Congress shall make no law respecting an establishment of religion"? The clause was only intended to stop the formation of a national Church. That's all!

At the time of the American Revolution, nine of the thirteen colonies had state churches. The Anglican Church was the established church in six states: Virginia, in the "lower counties" of New York, in Maryland, in South Carolina, in North Carolina "nominally," and in Georgia. In Massachusetts, Connecticut, and New Hampshire, the Congregational Church was the established state church. By the time of the Constitutional Convention in 1787, that number had whittled down to only five states with a state church. By that time "only

Georgia, South Carolina, Connecticut, Massachusetts, and New Hampshire had retained their religious establishments."[143] The last state church was that of Massachusetts, which lasted until 1833.

Thus, while the Constitution clearly prohibits the creation of a national church, it did not even prohibit a *state* church. They eventually withered away of their own accord, but they were never declared unconstitutional.

Historian Robert Cord, one-time professor of political science at Northeastern University, wrote a helpful book on this subject, entitled *Separation of Church and State: Historical Fact and Current Fiction.* Professor Cord tells of James Madison's first draft of the religion clause of the First Amendment:

> Madison's original wording of the Establishment of Religion Clause also supports my thesis concerning the separation of Church and State: "The Civil rights of none shall be abridged on account of religious belief of worship, nor shall any national religion be established, nor shall the full and equal rights of Conscience be in any manner, or on any pretext, infringed."[144]

Here we see from one of the Constitution's chief architects that the Establishment Clause means no national religion shall be established.

Because of the variety of Christian denominations in America, the founding fathers were wisely building safeguards so that no one sect would be able to lord it over the others. Madison said as such. On June 12, 1788, he said this to the Virginia Convention:

> Fortunately for this Commonwealth, a majority of the people are decidedly against any exclusive establishment. I believe it to be so in other states. There is not a shadow of right in the general government to intermeddle with religion. . . . The United States abound in such a variety of sects, that

it is a strong security against religious persecution, and it is sufficient to authorize a conclusion, that no one sect will ever be able to outnumber or depress the rest.[145]

These are almost shocking words to read today, in light of the continuous onslaught against any Christian expression in public.

The founders of this country never intended the First Amendment to be a hammer, chipping away at our religious freedoms blow by blow. They never intended that the First Amendment would be invoked to prevent a child from saying grace before his meal at school.

After examining the evidence, Professor Cord concludes there were three purposes to the First Amendment, according to those who drafted and adopted it. The first we've already discussed is that no national church was to be established. He mentions the other two aims:

> Second, it was designed to safeguard the right of freedom of conscience in religious beliefs against invasion solely by the national Government.
>
> Third, it was so constructed in order to allow the States, unimpeded, to deal with religious establishments and aid to religious institutions as they saw fit.
>
> There appears to be no historical evidence that the First Amendment was intended to preclude Federal governmental aid to religion when it was provided on a nondiscriminatory basis. Nor does there appear to be any historical evidence that the First Amendment was intended to provide an absolute separation or independence of religion and the national state. The actions of the early Congresses and Presidents, in fact, suggest quite the opposite. For example, James Madison, who again played an important role in the writing of the Constitution, served on the "Committee that recommended the Congressional

Chaplain system."[146]

Thus, the First Amendment as understood by the founders of this country is not at all what we see being imposed on us today, mostly by the courts. What is taught in the law schools today for the most part is the new interpretation—that the founders intended no public acknowledgement of God.

Furthermore, our founding fathers never intended to hinder in any way the affairs of the Church. We saw at the very beginning of this chapter a quote from George Washington, where he noted, in a letter dated May 10, 1789, to the United Baptist Churches in Virginia, that if he thought the Constitution would "possibly endanger the religious rights of any ecclesiastical Society," then he absolutely would not have signed the document. Here's the man who presided over the convention and all its proceedings, objecting to the idea that the Constitution could be used against churches.

I don't think our first president would be a fan of the ACLU and their kind. He also said, in another letter to a religious body (the Synod of the Dutch Reformed Church in North America): "true religion affords to government its surest support."[147]

MISINTERPRETATION OF THE FIRST AMENDMENT

In light of all these things, where did we go astray? How have things become so twisted around? Much of the change began with a 1947 Supreme Court decision, a decision that was to have far-reaching implications long after the particulars were well-known.

The turning point in American jurisprudence in church-state matters was the 1947 *Everson v. Board of Education* decision. Justice Hugo Black applied for the first time the "separation of Church and State" concept to the First Amendment. He took a private letter from Thomas Jefferson to the Danbury Baptists (written January 1, 1802) out of context and said that the Constitution erects a "high and impregnable" wall between church and state. *Time* Magazine points out: "That ruling marked a sharp separationist turn in court thinking.

It unleashed a torrent of litigation that continues to flood courtrooms [64] years later. And in a succession of cases, the court drew the line ever more strictly."[148]

Over time, this interpretation came to gain wide circulation, so much so that, again, the average person today most likely thinks that the Constitution even teaches "the separation of Church and State." What this misinterpretation of the First Amendment has done is to effectively turn the First Amendment against religion, instead of protecting religion as it was designed to do.

As the effect of the *Everson* decision began to be felt, it achieved its zenith under the Warren Court. In 1962 and 1963 came the infamous school prayer decisions, *Engel v. Vitale, Abington v. Schempp* and *Murray v. Curlett.* The Court could not tolerate any acknowledgment of God by the state, or its agents—in this case, teachers. The fallout of these decisions has been horrendous. Often, principals and administrators have taken these and other High Court decisions to ridiculous lengths.

In its first prayer decision on June 17, 1962, *Engel v. Vitale,* the Supreme Court ruled this innocuous prayer unconstitutional: "Almighty God, we acknowledge our dependence upon Thee, and we beg Thy blessing upon us, our parents, our teachers and our country."[149] At that time, only one Supreme Court Justice dissented (and Byron White, new to the court, didn't vote). "I think this decision is wrong,"[150] said the lone dissenter, Justice Potter Stewart. At that time, *Newsweek* quoted Stewart as saying he couldn't see how "'an official religion' is established by letting those who want to say a prayer to say it. Citing several examples of U.S. institutions that invoke prayer (including the Supreme Court itself, which opens with the words, 'God save the United States and this honorable Court'), the Ohio jurist summed up his attitude with a line from a ten-year-old Court decision [*Zorach v. Clauson*]: 'We are a religious people whose institutions presuppose a Supreme Being.'"[151]

The only way that the modern secularist can come to the conclusion that the founders of this country intended a purely secular state, where the state is "neutral" toward religion is by selective history. They base their decisions on a few selected passages from our history and ignore a mountain of evidence to the contrary.

INSIGHTS FROM OUR FORMER CHIEF JUSTICE

One man who disagreed with this misinterpretation of the First Amendment was the former Chief Justice of the U.S. Supreme Court, William Rehnquist. He said this in his brilliant dissent of a case ruling against a moment of silence, *Wallace v. Jaffree* (1984):

> It is impossible to build sound constitutional doctrine upon a mistaken understanding of constitutional history, but unfortunately the Establishment Clause has been expressly freighted with Jefferson's misleading metaphor for nearly 40 years. Thomas Jefferson was, of course, in France at the time the constitutional Amendments known as the Bill of Rights were passed by Congress and ratified by the States. His letter to the Danbury Baptist Association was a short note of courtesy, written 14 years after the Amendments were passed by Congress. He would seem to any detached observer as a less than ideal source of contemporary history as to the meaning of the Religion Clauses of the First Amendment.... The "wall of separation between church and State" is a metaphor based on bad history, a metaphor which has proved useless as a guide to judging. It should be frankly and explicitly abandoned.... The true meaning of the Establishment Clause can only be seen in its history.... The Framers intended the Establishment Clause to prohibit the designation of any church as a "national" one. The Clause was also designed to stop the Federal Government from asserting a preference for one religious denomination or sect over others. Given the "incorporation" of the Establishment Clause as against the States via the Fourteenth Amendment

in *Everson,* States are prohibited as well from establishing a religion or discriminating between sects. As its history abundantly shows, however, nothing in the Establishment Clause requires government to be strictly neutral between religion and irreligion, nor does that Clause prohibit Congress or the States from pursuing legitimate secular ends through nondiscriminatory sectarian means....[152]

This dissent is incredible. Here, one of our great legal minds is saying that the current interpretation of religion in public is a wrong one that continues to wreak legal havoc on the Constitution. And I would add: havoc on our society.

What he said bears repeating: "The 'wall of separation between church and State' is a metaphor based on bad history, a metaphor which has proved useless as a guide to judging. It should be frankly and explicitly abandoned." Would that more judges, law professors, teachers, and principals would follow his advice.

We see the loss of religious liberty in all sorts of ways in our culture. But let's look at an example from last year's Christmas season.

'TIS THE SEASON TO JETTISON REASON?

For the last couple of decades, Senator Jim Inhofe has ridden a horse in the Tulsa Christmas parade, year after year. And he has loved it. With a twinkle in his eyes, he proudly says, "There are only two things I do well. Ride horses and fly planes."[153] He was all set to ride in the parade last year for the nth time, when he found out that they had dropped "Christmas" from the name of the parade. Now it's just the "holiday" parade. He hadn't realized it until he showed up last year. So he said then (and he says now), "I'm not riding in this."

I had the privilege of interviewing Sen. Inhofe on a variety of issues about a year ago for *The Coral Hour* (now *Truth That Transforms with Dr. D. James Kennedy*). In his interview, he happened to mention his recent decision to boycott the parade because of the name change—which is just one more example of what's been called the war on Christmas. Said the Senator, "Now they're making a big issue in Tulsa, Oklahoma, that I'm refusing to ride, as I've done for decades, in the Christmas parade because they took Jesus out of the Christmas parade. Well, if He goes, I go."[154]

If more people were courageous like Sen. Inhofe, we'd probably not see the further secularization of the Christmas season. Perhaps, I should say "holiday season." An interesting irony of the anti-Christmas forces that use the word holiday is the origin of the word....holiday is a contraction of holy day—that's why there's only one "L" in holiday . . . I wonder what "holy day" that would be referring to?

Every year, like clockwork, the Grinches come out of the woodwork in their war against Christmas.

For example, a group of atheists in New York City paid for a billboard ad with an anti-Christmas message: "You know it's a myth. This season celebrate reason." Well, I celebrate both Christmas and reason, and I know plenty of intellectuals who do so as well. Just try struggling through one page of St. Thomas Aquinas' *Summa Theologica* and tell me that faith and reason are incompatible. The great appeal of Christmas is that the message is simple enough to satisfy people with all IQ levels.

It is strange when you consider how threatening a manger scene is to some in our society today. It represents a baby! A baby that escaped the clutches of King Herod. A baby that inspires acts of mercy and love all over the world. A baby that received gifts from the wise men—inspiring the annual season of gift-giving. Frankly, I think all the retailers in this country should assemble on December 26 each year, hold hands, and sing, "What a friend we have in Jesus."

And yet, the war on Christmas goes on unabated. It's as if He is not invited to His own birthday party. A few years ago, children at the Ridgeway Elementary School in Dodgeville, Wisconsin, performing in a "winter program," were to sing the melody of "Silent Night," but with the words, "Cold in the night, no one in sight, winter winds whirl and bite, how I wish

I were happy and warm, safe with my family out of the storm." The school officials didn't dare offend anyone with the original words of the classic carol.

But at the end of the day, nothing can stop Christmas. After all, we're talking about the religion of the catacombs.

Even the Grinch in the contemporary tale couldn't stop Christmas. Nor can the "holiday parade" organizers of Tulsa, Oklahoma. It's just too bad that we find that the war on Christmas is now reaching even into a place like Tulsa. New York City I can understand, but Tulsa? With each passing year, it seems that the only principle getting stronger in our culture is the ABC principle—Anything But Christ.

Hopefully, the city officials in Tulsa will not jettison reason, but come to their senses and relent, so that the good senator will be able to saddle up this year to celebrate Christmas, as in times past.

CONCLUSION

About 75 years after the Revolutionary War, some critics challenged the concept that America is a Christian nation—it was a challenge as to what the First Amendment meant regarding religion. The U.S. Congress appointed a commission to study the issue. Congressman Meacham of the House Judiciary Committee submitted his detailed report to the Congress on March 27, 1854, with a resounding "Yes" to the thesis. He documents in detail after detail the Christian origins of the country. Note what he said about Christianity and the American War for Independence: "Had the people, during the Revolution, had a suspicion of any attempt to war against Christianity, that Revolution would have been strangled in its cradle."[155]

As we see more and more attempts to separate God from the public square, we will also see an increased attempt of the state to meddle in the affairs of the Church—not only determining who can be hired, but, perhaps even interfering with what can be said in the pulpits. This may sound far-fetched, but I keep thinking of the recent example from a small church in an obscure part of Sweden, where the pastor lovingly said what the Bible says about homosexuality. A tape of his sermon was sent to the police, who listened to it and then determined that he had committed a hate crime for saying homosexuality was a sin. The pastor was sentenced to jail, and only when attorneys from the American legal group, the Alliance Defense Fund (that Dr. Kennedy co-founded), went over to Sweden and successfully defended his case was he spared from prison.

The Establishment Clause was supposed to protect the conscience of the individual and limit Congress. Today's misinterpretation limits the free exercise of conscience and empowers the state to control religion.

CHAPTER FIVE

Religion and Morality are "Indispensible Supports"

*We have no government armed
with power capable of contending with human
passions unbridled by morality and religion.
Avarice, ambition, revenge, or gallantry, would break
the strongest cords of our Constitution as a whale
goes through a net. Our Constitution was made
only for a moral and religious people. It is wholly
inadequate to the government of any other.*[156]

John Adams

George Washington, the father of our country, said in his Farewell Address that "religion and morality" were "indispensible supports" to our "political prosperity." Similarly, John Adams said that our Constitution was designed for a virtuous people—"a moral and religious people." If the people neglect morality and religion (Christianity), then it won't work.[157]

Why do we see the breakdown in modern America? Because, as a nation, we are largely ignoring the true source of morality, which is religion—namely Christianity. When the founders referred to "religion," as in the Washington and Adams' quotes above, they are talking about Christianity.

As we have seen, 99.8 percent of the people in this country as late as 1776, 150 plus years after the Pilgrims landed here, professed themselves to be Christians. Specifically, that breaks down to 98.4% Protestant and 1.4% Roman Catholic.[158]

THE BIBLE AND THE FOUNDING ERA

A number of years ago, Charles S. Hyneman and Donald S. Lutz, two political science professors, conducted a major study of key documents from America's founding era (1760-1805). They examined 15,000 documents, including several thousand books, looking specifically for their political content. Even more specifically, they were looking to see what sources were cited in these political volumes, monographs, pamphlets, newspaper articles, and so on. They found 3,154 citations or references to other sources.

Of these more than 3,000 citations, they found that the source quoted or cited the most was the Holy Bible. Thirty-four percent of these citations came from the Judeo-Christian Scriptures.[159] Speaking of the documents in the Hyneman and Lutz study, David Barton points out, "Four times more often than they quote any individual, they quote the Bible."[160]

The top three human authors cited were Montesquieu (8.3% of the citations), Sir William Blackstone (7.9%), and John Locke (2.9%). Interestingly, these three were professing Christians, who had a Christian world-and-life view. Their views on politics, government and law were influenced directly and positively by the Bible.

Dr. Lutz wrote *The Origins of American Constitutionalism,* a great book that documents the link between Christian influences—including the biblical concept of covenant—and America's second key founding document. Dr. Lutz's research has been invaluable in modern times to a proper understanding of our nation's true history and the Christian roots of America.

MONTESQUIEU

Baron Charles Louis Joseph de Secondat Montesquieu (1689-1755) was a French political scientist. He is often categorized as an "Enlightenment thinker," as are Blackstone and Locke. However, as some political scientists point out, there are two basic types of Enlightenment thinkers—Christian and anti-Christian. All three of these writers are in the former category, whereas David Hume, Rousseau, and Voltaire are in the latter category.

Montesquieu is generally credited with being the source the founders drew from for the separation of powers into three specific branches of government (executive, legislative, judicial). Since this view arose in the Judeo-Christian tradition, it is interesting to note that 700 years before Christ, the Hebrew prophet Isaiah hints at the same idea. He says, "For the Lord is our Judge, the Lord is our lawgiver, the Lord is our king" (Isaiah 33:22).

Montesquieu notes that Christian morality has political implications. In Book XXIV of *The Spirit of the Laws,* Montesquieu wrote:

> I have always respected religion; the morality of the Gospel is the noblest gift ever bestowed by God on man. We shall see that we owe to Christianity, in government, a certain political law, and in war a certain law of nations—benefits which human nature can never sufficiently acknowledge.
>
> The principles of Christianity, deeply engraved on the heart, would be infinitely more powerful

than the false honor of monarchies, than the humane virtues of republics, or the servile fear of despotic states.

It is the Christian religion that, in spite of the extent of empire and the influence of climate, has hindered despotic power from being established in Ethiopia, and has carried into the heart of Africa the manners and laws of Europe.[161]

Montesquieu goes on to note the contrast between Christianity and Islam, especially as it relates to political power:

The Christian religion is a stranger to mere despotic power. The mildness so frequently recommended in the Gospel is incompatible with the despotic rage with which a prince punishes his subjects, and exercises himself in cruelty. . . .

A moderate Government is most agreeable to the Christian Religion, and a despotic Government to the Mahommedan. . . . While the Mahommedan princes incessantly give or receive death, the religion of the Christians renders their princes less timid, and consequently less cruel.[162]

I showed this quote to a friend who said, "Isn't that just common knowledge?" But I said, "Look at what Rosie O'Donnell said famously on *The View* a few years ago: 'Radical Christianity is just as threatening as radical Islam in a country like America.'"[163] The amazing thing about her statement is that the audience applauded her remark, as if it were true. Unfortunately, it isn't necessarily common knowledge that Christianity tends to less cruel governments, whereas Islamic states can often be despotic. By the way, I'm sure Rosie would not want to live any time soon in a country where they imposed strict Islamic law.

BLACKSTONE

A very influential thinker, Sir William Blackstone (1723-1780) was a British jurist, who wrote a four volume series on the laws of his country, *Commentary on the Laws of England*. Abraham Lincoln learned the law by reading a second-hand copy of one of Blackstone's volumes.

In a booklet entitled, *Our Legal Heritage*, former Alabama Chief Justice Moore writes: "Even today, Blackstone's Commentaries are frequently cited by the United States Supreme Court." Justice Moore points out that in 1775, Edmund Burke rose up in Parliament to explain why it was that America had such a "fierce spirit of liberty." He pointed out that there was a widespread interest in law and that Blackstone's *Commentaries on the Laws of England* were perhaps more popular in the colonies than they were in Britain. Said Burke:

> In no country perhaps in the world is the law so general a study . . . But all who read, and most do read, endeavor to obtain some smattering in that science. I have been told by an eminent bookseller that in no branch of business, after tracts of popular devotion, were so many books as those on the law exported to the plantations. The colonists have now fallen into the way of printing them for their own use. I hear that they have sold nearly as many Blackstone's Commentaries in America as in England.[164]

Blackstone held that God is the source of law. He created His world with physical laws governing it. Blackstone clarifies further:

> This will of his Maker is called the law of nature. For as God, when He created matter, and endued it with a principle of mobility, established certain rules for the perpetual direction of that motion; so, when He created man, and endued him with free will to conduct himself in all parts of life, He laid down certain immutable laws of human nature, whereby that free will is in some degree regulated and restrained, and gave him also the faculty of reason to discover the purport of those laws.[165]

Not only did God create physical laws in the universe, He also created moral laws that are just as binding and unchangeable. Furthermore, Blackstone shows that God's laws reflect His infinite wisdom:

> But as He is also a Being of infinite wisdom, He has laid down only such laws as were founded in those relations of justice, that existed in the nature of things antecedent to any positive precept. These are the eternal, immutable laws of good and evil, to which the Creator Himself in all his Dispensations conforms; and which He has enabled human reason to discover, so far as they are necessary for the conduct of human actions. Such among others, are these principles: that we should live honestly, should hurt nobody, and should render to everyone his due; to which three general precepts Justinian has reduced the whole doctrine of law. . . .[166]

Blackstone is saying that the golden rule—which, by the way, first came from the lips of Jesus Christ (Matthew 7:12)—is the summary of God's moral law.

Blackstone went on to speak of the law of nature and the revealed law—that is, what we find in Holy Scripture: "Upon these two foundations, the law of nature and the law of revelation, depend all human laws; that is to say, no human laws should be suffered to contradict these."[167] So, when the founders talked about how religion and morality are important to the American people, they were referring to explicitly Christian concepts.

LOCKE

As we saw earlier, John Locke (1632-1704) was an English political scientist who would later have a profound impact on the founders, including Jefferson. In *The Second Treatise on Civil Government*, 1690, John Locke wrote,

> Human Laws are measures in respect of Men whose

> Actions they must direct, albeit such measures they
> are as have also their higher Rules to be measured
> by, which Rules are two, the Law of God, and
> the Law of Nature; so that Laws Human must be
> made according to the general Laws of Nature,
> and without contradiction to any positive Law of
> Scripture, otherwise they are ill made.[168]

When we deal with issues of morality, we ultimately wonder, who is to say what is right or wrong? According to John Locke, a source of great importance to America's founders, God determines what is right or wrong. How do we find out what God says? Through the Scriptures.

THE FOUNDERS' BELIEF IN VIRTUE

The founders intended that America would be moral. They also intended that this would be accomplished through voluntary religion—by which they meant Christianity. Thomas Jefferson once said, "Of all the systems of morality, ancient or modern, which have come under my observation, none appear to me so pure as that of Jesus."[169]

Dr. Lutz points out that "The concept of virtue was central to politics throughout the seventeenth and eighteenth centuries in America."[170] Virtue, of course, was defined with a biblical criterion, notes Lutz. "In one sense, virtue meant following God's law as found in the Bible. One who did not lie, steal, or fornicate, but who adhered to the golden rule was a virtuous person."[171] Lutz adds, "And the most fundamental assumption is that *the American people are a virtuous people.*"[172]

Lutz cites a typical statement from a sermon from that time—this one being from Phillips Payson, minister of the town of Dorchester, Massachusetts: "The voice of reason and the voice of God both teach us that the great object or end of government is the public good."[173] Government was not viewed as beyond God's purview or will.

Dr. Lutz even points out that without the belief in the people being religious (Christian) and moral, the founders might not have crafted our particular government: "Without the belief in a virtuous people, the federal republic would not have been tried."[174]

Benjamin Franklin noted in a letter dated April 17, 1787, a month before the Constitutional convention, "Only a virtuous people are capable of freedom. As nations become corrupt and vicious, they have more need of masters."[175]   Virtue does not come on its own. Virtue grows out of religious belief and practice. As Jesus put it, a good tree bears good fruit, a bad tree, bad fruit. Again, Dr. Lutz says: "American political thought had developed from radical Protestant theology, and thus political virtue had a religious base."[176]

The one belief, as Dr. Lutz points out, that even religious and non-religious founders of America shared was the importance of good works. As Christians, we are not saved *by* good works. But we are saved *unto* good works. It is faith alone that saves us, but that faith is not alone; if it's real, it will produce good fruit. Here's Dr. Lutz:

> An interesting aspect of this dual thrust is that religious and secular thinkers could agree on what kind of behavior was essential. For instance, many public documents, including half a dozen state constitutions, listed the following virtues: justice, moderation, temperance, industry, frugality, and honesty. Temperance was the religious equivalent of moderation, crucial virtues for a people hoping to achieve national economic independence and develop a strong economy, but American Calvinistic Christians also saw them as religious virtues.[177]

As Jesus put it: By their fruits, you shall know them.

To the Americans, the goal of government was the public good. Since most of them were Calvinists, industry and frugality were viewed as religious virtues. Benjamin Franklin can be viewed as a symbol of this type of American colonial belief in virtue. Although raised in Calvinistic Boston, apparently, he did not believe in the doctrines of the historic faith. Yet he believed deeply in its values. To borrow a phrase from Dr. Paul Jehle, we might say that Franklin liked the fruit of Calvinistic Christianity, while rejecting its root.

Benjamin Franklin reflects well the notion (which was reinforced in the newspapers at the time and taught in the schools, also) that Scripture is the source of national morality. He stated:

> A Bible and a newspaper in every house, a good school in every district—all studied and appreciated as they merit—are the principal support of virtue, morality, and civil liberty. A nation of well informed men who have been taught to know and prize the rights which God has given them cannot be enslaved. It is in the region of ignorance that tyranny begins.
>
> God grant that not only the Love of Liberty but a thorough knowledge of the rights of man may pervade all the nation.[178]

One of the reasons we're in trouble today is because the newspaper—the media— and the schools teach messages contrary to the Bible—not in favor of it.

Ben Franklin went on to say that an outgrowth of our God-given rights is that we will be happy if we are moral: "Freedom is not a gift bestowed upon us by other men, but a right that belongs to us by the laws of God and nature. Without virtue, man can have no happiness. Virtue alone is sufficient to make a man great, glorious and happy."[179]

Furthermore, we must understand that Franklin viewed virtue essentially as a public good. On January 1, 1769, Benjamin Franklin corresponded with Lord James:

> The moral character and happiness of mankind are so interwoven with the operation of government, and the progress of the arts and sciences is so dependent on the nature of our political institutions, that it is essential to the advancement of civilized society to give ample discussion to these topics.[180]

We should be very clear here to note that moralism does not save. Only the blood of Jesus saves. If Ben Franklin was under the false impression that his virtues were good enough to bring him to God, he was mistaken. I'm sure many of his virtues and morals were essentially piggy-backed from his Christian upbringing. Only trusting in Jesus Christ, who died for sinners on the Cross, can save us.

Yet the Gospel often has a positive and enduring influence in a culture—even on those who don't believe, yet absorb and practice Christian values and morals. It's my understanding that Franklin may have belonged in that category.

However, as we'll see in a later chapter, he also believed strongly in a prayer-answering God, removing Franklin from the category of a Deist. (A Deist believes in a clock-maker god who made the world, wound it all up, and essentially left it to its own devices. A Deist could not affirm the incarnation of Jesus nor a personal God who would answer prayer.)

The founders of America believed that our Constitution would work for a moral and religious (Christian) people who were free to practice their religion as they see fit. As Franklin once famously said (to paraphrase him): We have given you a republic, if you can keep it. Voluntary religion (Christianity) was one of the major means of keeping it.

Jump ahead nearly a century and we find our 16th president, Abraham Lincoln, who was clearly a student of the Scriptures, declaring when he received the gift of a Bible: "In regard to this great book, I have but to say, it is the best gift God has given to men. All the good the Savior gave to the world was communicated through this book. But for it, we could not know right from wrong."[181] How do we discern right from wrong? By studying the Scriptures.

Neither Ben Franklin nor Abraham Lincoln would be pleased with what has happened today. In the last several decades, the Supreme Court, our educational establishment, and other elites have essentially banished God and godly beliefs from the public square. Through a misinterpretation of the Constitution, God has been effectively dismissed from the schools, from the courtroom, from some of the halls of government. What has been the effect of all this? We read about it everyday. We are fast approaching the description found in the book of Judges in the midst of Israel's Dark Ages, if you will: "In those days there was no king in Israel; everyone did what was right in his own eyes (Judges 17:6).

Each person today in America decides what's right and what's wrong. The only sin in this milieu is judging someone else for sinning. Who are you to say that there is a real right or real wrong?

TRAGIC RESULTS OF GODLESSNESS

What have been the results of removing God from the public life from America? Here's just one disturbing example to explore—public brawls.

Recently, total strangers have been fighting each other, usually in fast food restaurants. These tragic incidents have been caught on video, have been posted on the Internet, and "have gone viral."

This has happened at McDonald's, at Burger King, at IHOP, at Denny's. Even on the subway, total strangers have been fighting each other. Some of these seem to be racially motivated. Others not.

The ancient Christians used to talk about the Seven Deadly Sins—one of which was anger. Now, this deadly sin is proving deadly once again. . .or nearly deadly.

Recently, two female teenage patrons of McDonald's in Baltimore County allegedly beat up a stranger, who suffered an epileptic seizure and was rushed to the hospital. At a Panama City, Florida, Burger King, another patron had a fit of uncontrolled anger, unleashing mayhem by hitting people and destroying property. Apparently, she had had a conflict with an employee while in the drive-through, so she reportedly came storming in and began throwing things around, striking an employee or two, and even breaking some things—like a $3,800 LED screen. All of this was caught on video tape, probably from another customer with a cell phone.

The video of the rampage has become quite a hit on YouTube. The tragedy is that these types of incidents are becoming more and more common in America, as we descend into incivility.

Are these brawls becoming so common because of the omnipresence of cell phones with the capability to capture video? Or are they becoming common because of the total breakdown of morality? Whatever the case, there is no doubt that we're seeing a total breakdown of morality in our culture.

What went wrong?

Our nation's founders said that our freedoms are predicated on an ability to remain virtuous, and they said that morality was predicated on religion—religion on a voluntary basis. John Adams, our second president, said (as we noted above) that our constitution will only work for a moral and religious people. "It is wholly inadequate to the government of any other."

Another founding father, Gouverneur Morris, is not so well known today. But he spoke more than any other framer at the Constitutional convention. He even wrote major portions of the Constitution, including the preamble ("We the people . . ."). Morris said, "Religion is the only solid basis of good morals; therefore education should teach the precepts of religion, and the duties of man toward God."[182] But now we're told it's unconstitutional to do so.

Of course, these aspects of our true history have been jettisoned by the politically correct elites who hold the reins of power in media, academia, and government. This new secular establishment has spent 50 years driving out every vestige of religion from public life. Now we're reaping what we've sown.

Through groups like the ACLU, which has made sure that no sneaky remnant of religion (well, actually Christianity) is allowed in the public realm, we've been having it the ACLU's way in America. And that's precisely the problem. Tragically, as God and religious principles are driven out further and further from the public schools, we can expect more fits of rage to take place at fast food establishments and elsewhere. Based on a faulty reading of the Constitution, the Bible is no longer allowed in the public sphere, and we're beginning to see how ugly life is without its positive influence.

A LESSON FROM THE OTHER SIDE OF THE POND

We Americans can learn even from England's recent "Lord of the Flies" mayhem that took place in the summer of 2011. Looters and rioters ran loose for days in that great country, leaving in their wake a few people dead, many businesses destroyed, hundreds arrested, and untold damage.

A friend of mine from south England told me at the gym at the time of the riots, "To see what's happening now makes me ashamed to be a Brit."

This recent episode in England reminds me of a conversation I had during the L. A. riots of 1992. My brother has an office high atop Los Angeles with a great view, and he and I were on the phone. He would say, "Oh, there's another fire over there. And another one on that side." Then he said something that shocked me, coming from him.

He said, "It's all these kids without religion."

"But," I said, referring to his views at that time, "You're an atheist. How can you say that?"

He said, "I know. But it's still true"—in other words, that these were kids without religion.

What we saw on the streets of England was man's base nature coming through without restraint. The Good Book has many sober reminders of the reality of human nature. "The heart is desperately wicked, who can understand it?" we read in Scripture.

G.K. Chesterton is alleged to have said that since the dawn of recorded history, we have had 6,500 years of empirical evidence of the doctrine of original sin. As Cassius says in Shakespeare's *Julius Caesar*, "The fault, Dear Brutus, is not in our stars, but in ourselves. . . ."

What we see before our very eyes is that the traditional supports of our society are crumbling. We thought we could be moral and good without God. But incidents like the British riots are the result of a generation (or more) without biblical teaching.

But obviously not everyone shares these opinions. Do they assume that human beings will just be good on their own? Many years ago, media mogul Ted Turner said that the Ten Commandments are obsolete, and they ought to be abandoned. He came up with a not-so-modest alternative, which he called "the Ten Voluntary Initiatives."

When speaking before various groups, I have asked the audience if they remember this story. Occasionally a hand or two might go up. Then I have asked them, if they remembered the story, can they remember any items on his list? The answer is always negative.

No, not one.

Anybody can make any list of rights or wrongs they want to, but accountability is the key. Ted Turner is not the one before whom we'll give an account on the Day of Reckoning.

Those kids "without religion" looting on the streets of Great Britain remind me of Dostoyevsky's famous statement (from *The Brothers Karamazov*): "...everything is permitted... since there is no infinite God, there's no such thing as virtue either, and there's no need for it at all."[183]

CONCLUSION

Since we're sinful in our natures, we need forgiveness and a new nature. Only Christ can do that. Most of the founders seemed to understand that. They understood the critical role that Christianity played in causing such regeneration. They never intended to deliver to us the godless public square we now have to deal with.

Rev. Martin Luther King, Jr. once said that in his opinion, it was not possible to legislate morality. (Many would counter-argue that all legislation reflects someone's morality. The question is: Whose morality will prevail?) But Dr. King went on to say, "While the law cannot change the heart, it can certainly restrain the heartless."[184]

Our slide into further immorality will only continue unless

more and more Americans come to embrace the Gospel and then live out their faith. Robert Charles Winthrop, who served as Speaker of the U.S. House of Representatives, said this to the Massachusetts Bible Society in Boston on May 28, 1849:

> All societies of men must be governed in some way or other. The less they have of stringent State Government, the more they must have of individual self-government. The less they rely on public law or physical force, the more they must rely on private moral restraint.
>
> Men, in a word, must necessarily be controlled either by a power within them, or a power without them; either by the Word of God, or by the strong arm of man; either by the Bible or by the bayonet.[185]

CHAPTER SIX

Imitation of Christ— "The Divine Author of Our Blessed Religion"

I now make it my earnest prayer…
that he would most graciously be pleased to dispose
us all, to do Justice, to love mercy, and to demean
ourselves with that Charity, humility and pacific
temper of mind, which were the Characteristics
of the Divine Author of our blessed Religion,
and without an humble imitationof whose
example in these things, we can never
hope to be a happy Nation.[186]

George Washington

George Washington, the father of our country, said that we can never hope to be a happy nation unless we imitate the Savior. After the war, but before the official treaty ending the conflict, Commander-in-Chief Washington sent a letter to the governors of the thirteen states. It was a famous letter, dated June 13, 1783, and is called the "Circular to the States." Near the end of this circular, Washington said that he prayed we will all learn to imitate Jesus Christ. This is exactly how he worded it:

> I now make it my earnest prayer, that God would have you, and the State over which you preside, in his holy protection, that he would incline the hearts of the Citizens to cultivate a spirit of subordination and obedience to Government, to entertain a brotherly affection and love for one another, for their fellow Citizens of the United States at large, and particularly for their brethren who have served in the Field, and finally, that he would most graciously be pleased to dispose us all, to do Justice, to love mercy, and to demean ourselves with that Charity, humility and pacific temper of mind, which were the Characteristics of the Divine Author of our blessed Religion, and without an humble imitation of whose example in these things, we can never hope to be a happy Nation.[187]

One of the great things we can learn from the father of our nation is that the more the nation imitates Jesus, the happier we will be.

This is not the only place where he spoke of the importance of imitating Christ. For example, one time a delegation of Delaware Indian Chiefs came to see him and ask him how their young men could learn from the ways of the British settlers. This was in 1779. Washington told them, "You do well to wish to learn our arts and ways of life, and above all, the religion of Jesus Christ."[188] He added an interesting post-script to his message: "Congress will do everything they can to assist you in this wise intention."

Here we have George Washington, a leading (if not the leading) founding father of America, saying that Indians would do well to imitate Jesus Christ. He also is saying that Congress would help them in the goal to learn more about the religion of Jesus.

But surely this flies in the face of the "separation of church and state"—someone may object. The idea of the separation of church and state (especially the separation of God and state) was not the prevailing view during the founding era. It is more of a recent invention. The founders did not want any one Christian denomination "by law established" to be our national state church. They certainly didn't want atheism (essentially unknown to the vast majority of them) to be our national "religion."

The very men who gave us the First Amendment violated it left and right—if, by it, they meant the strict separation of God and state. That is not what they meant, as we have seen in an earlier chapter. In this chapter we want to focus on how Washington encouraged his countrymen—and now us—to imitate Jesus.

What difference does it make when one follows Christ versus rejecting Him? This is the key to our national and personal problems today, as it was at the founding of our nation. Let's look at an interesting contrast.

THE DIFFERENCE JESUS MAKES

A son is supposed to obey his mother. That's not true, though, when your mother is the best known atheist in America. Here's a case where a young man eventually chose to imitate Christ, while his mother reviled Him.

William J. Murray's mother was the notorious atheist, Madalyn Murray O'Hair. One of the defining moments in her life, when her atheism became solidified, happened when she ran outside during a thunderstorm and defied God—if there was one—to strike her dead right then and there. He chose not to. "You see, you see." she exclaimed, "I've proved irrefutably that God does not exist."[189]

My comment to Madalyn would be fourfold: 1) God in His sovereignty chooses not to answer the prideful prayers of His creatures; 2) God in His sovereignty chooses whom He will, even to bring judgment on nations. Perhaps He has used the militant anti-Christian movement she helped mobilize to arouse portions of His sleeping Church; 3) God in His mercy chose not to smite her because of His mercy, that she might receive the opportunity to repent—she lived for at least three decades after this incident; and 4) she was pregnant at the time, and inside her was William J. Murray, one of the Lord's future servants. If God answered her pitiful, little rebellious prayer, William wouldn't be here to remind us to return to God.

I once interviewed Bill for *The Coral Ridge Hour* (now *Truth That Transforms with Dr. D. James Kennedy*) and asked him how it was that he came to believe in God. The gist of his answer was that life was so miserable growing up in such an anti-God environment that it made him open to hearing the Gospel. After being exposed to a fiery form of atheism all his life, William J. Murray came to a realization: "*There has to be a God, because there certainly is a devil. I have met him, talked to him, and touched him. He is the personification of evil.*"[190]

He eventually submitted to Christ the King, after reading the Gospel of Luke. Why would an atheist read that or any other Gospel? Murray had read the novel *Dear and Glorious Physician* by Taylor Caldwell. At the end of the book, she refers her readers to the Gospel of Luke for more information. So he picked it up. By that time he was so sick of the dysfunctional world of atheism he had experienced in his family that he was open to the message of Christ.[191] Today he is a powerful evangelist and also an advocate of allowing God back into the public schools—the very man, who as a boy, had been at the center of *Murray vs. Curlett* (1963), one of the key Supreme Court anti-school-prayer decisions.

The mother died, it would seem, in an unrepentant state. Apparently, she trusted a man fresh out of prison who convinced her to, in effect, embezzle some $600,000 worth of assets from her atheist empire. Then he allegedly robbed her and murdered her, along with Bill's half-brother, Jon Murray, and Bill's daughter, Robin Murray, who had been associated with Madalyn since childhood. Their remains weren't discovered until five to six years after their sudden disappearance. One can only imagine the grisly circumstances in which she and her son and granddaughter died.

What happens to lifelong atheists who explicitly refuse the grace of Jesus Christ and encourage others to do so? Some might die in gruesome circumstances, as Madalyn did. Others might die in peace in luxurious surroundings. Their eternal end remains the same.

The interesting contrast between Bill and his mother is that one chose to imitate Christ. The other chose not to. Bill's mother chose poorly.

PATRICK HENRY

Many of our founding fathers chose to imitate Jesus. David Barton points out that of the 250 or so men we call founding fathers, only a small handful—12 at most—would have questionable religious views. The vast majority of them were active church-goers and church leaders—at churches which proclaimed the Trinity and the other key doctrines of the historical Christian faith.

In his Last Will and Testament, Patrick Henry pointed to the teachings of the New Testament as he included this final bequest to his family:

> I have now disposed of all my property to my family; there is one thing more I wish I could give them, and that is the Christian religion. If they had that, and I had not given them one shilling, they would be rich, and if they had not that, and I had given them all the world, they would be poor. This is all the inheritance I give to my dear family. The religion of Christ will give them one which will make them rich indeed.[192]

We are not imitating Jesus these days. It seems as if we're doing everything we can to exclude Him from our lives.

THE GRACE OF JESUS CHRIST

I like going on secular talk shows to be the token "Christian guest." I don't know—maybe I'm just a glutton for punishment. But I enjoy the intellectual give-and-take. For example, I have appeared on *Politically Incorrect with Bill Maher* four times. Whatever confidence I have in appearing on these shows comes from knowing the overall truth of Christianity; I also remind myself that the people I talk with are human beings like me—they put their pants on one leg at a time.

When I was a guest on one such show in Miami, an interesting exchange came during one of the commercial breaks. The hostess (who was Jewish, unbelieving, and downright hostile) lit up a cigarette, looked at me, and said, "Jesus? Shmesus. Means absolutely nothing to me and my life." Then she blew out her smoke—generally in my direction.

I responded, "Sandy, if you only knew, you'd realize that every beat of your heart was by the grace of Jesus Christ."

Boy, did that anger her. She glared at me, as if I had said something terrible—something like, I think rape should be legalized and abortion not.

Christian-bashers abound in our day, and they are constantly discouraging us from imitating Christ.

TO HIM WE SHALL GIVE AN ACCOUNT

But, the opinions of secular talk show hosts notwithstanding, Jesus Christ has a claim on the lives of each one of us. And to Him alone we shall all give an account of our lives one day.

In Psalm 2, David writes about the son of David. From a Christian perspective, it is clearly Jesus Christ being described here. If we understood things aright, we would see Christ exalted in heaven, His Father holding the Christian-bashers in derision.

Here's the text of Psalm 2:

Why do the nations conspire and the peoples plot in vain? The kings of the earth take their stand and the rulers gather together against the LORD and against his Anointed One. "Let us break their chains," they say, "and throw off their fetters." The One enthroned in heaven laughs; the Lord scoffs at them. Then he rebukes them in his anger and terrifies them in his wrath, saying, "I have installed my King on Zion, my holy hill." I will proclaim the decree of the LORD: He said to me, "You are my Son; today I have become your Father. Ask of me, and I will make the nations your inheritance, the ends of the earth your possession. You will rule them with an iron scepter; you will dash them to pieces like pottery." Therefore, you kings, be wise; be warned, you rulers of the earth. Serve the LORD with fear and rejoice with trembling. Kiss the Son, lest he be angry and you be destroyed in your way, for his wrath can flare up in a moment. Blessed are all who take refuge in him. (NIV)

Who has the upper hand in Psalm 2? Who is the victim? Who is the victor? Jesus Christ is the victor.

The passage above is from the New International Version. In verse 1, the King James Version uses the word "heathen" instead of the word "nations." It means the same—those who are decidedly not God's people. In David's time, of course, only the Jews were God's people. With the coming of Christ, however, believing Gentiles are included in God's kingdom.

The founders, generally, had a healthy fear of Christ. They generally "kissed the Son" —that is, paid Him homage.

Why do the heathen rage, asks Psalm 2. Why? Because they want to break His bonds asunder. They don't want anyone to rule over them. They don't want anyone to tell them that what they do is wrong. Jesus summed up in a sentence why so many people reject Him: "Light has come into the world, but men prefer darkness because their deeds are evil" (John 3:19). This is why people in our culture repeatedly vilify the religious right. They don't want anybody telling them that there is a right and a wrong. But as the Bible says, "There is no wisdom, no insight, no plan that can succeed against the LORD" (Proverbs 21:30).

MANY HEATHEN RAGING AT THIS TIME

There are many in our day who do not like the Christian gospel. They declare of Christ the King, "We will not have this man rule over us" (Luke 19:14). They likely have no idea that George Washington said that we'll never be a happy nation without imitating Jesus.

Those who hate the Gospel have a stronghold on some of the leading cultural influences of our time. So we see and hear a steady drumbeat of anti-Christian messages that are widely disseminated. There is a strong anti-Christian bias in our world today. Consider the following.

- A few years ago, at Florida Atlantic University in Boca Raton, a college less than half an hour away from where I live (where my daughter earned her BA and met her future husband), the theater department staged a blasphemous play, "Corpus Christi," featuring a homosexual Christ. When Christians and politicians spoke out about this misuse of taxpayers' money, the defenders of the play retorted that "academic freedom" was at stake.

- Taxpayers' money also funded anti-Christian blasphemy in New York City in recent years. There was the museum exhibit featuring the Virgin Mary with smears of elephant dung on the depiction. It deservedly earned the mayor's ire. Then there was "Yo Mama's Last Supper," featuring a naked black woman as Jesus. Former Mayor Rudy Giuliani decried this work as "disgusting" and "anti-Catholic." Because of these kinds of "art" funded at the public expense, he created a twenty-member panel, including some artists and including some clergymen, to deal with future exhibits.

- In a typical decision, a judge sided with the

ACLU to rule against a public display of the Ten Commandments on the steps of a Florida county courthouse.

Meanwhile, many conservative Christians have experienced the wrath of militant, homosexual protesters, who are anything but tolerant.

- At a visit to Dartmouth University, an ex-lesbian speaker, Yvette Schneider, had to receive a police escort to escape out the back door from the wrath of homosexual activists. I call such militant protesters "The Shock Troops of Tolerance." Her personal effects left at the podium had to be gathered up and brought to her later. She was brought to the police station for her own safety. As upset as Yvette may have been, the head of the Christian group, which had invited Yvette to speak in the first place, came to the police station "visibly shaken as she sobbed uncontrollably."

- In September 1998, when two rednecks killed homosexual Matthew Shepherd in Wyoming, the media never stopped commenting on it. It was instantly defined as a hate crime. A year later, in September 1999, a man shouting anti-Christian expletives barged into Wedgewood Baptist Church of Ft. Worth during a service filled with young people. He shot and killed seven. The media and Attorney General Reno never got around to calling this a "hate crime." They spoke as if the motives were unclear and went to the grave with the troubled shooter who shot himself, too. Few Americans have forgotten about Matthew Shepherd because it was so widely reported. Few have remembered the incident at Wedgewood, because it was so underreported (comparatively).

- Anti-Christian hostility even reaches the breakfast table. General Mills Cereal, maker of

Cheerios and Cinnamon Toast Crunch, offered millions of free CD-ROMs in select boxes of cereal. The compact discs had free games, dictionaries, and initially, Bibles. But after a few complaints, they apologized, claiming they didn't realize the Bible was a part of the package. In tolerant America, there's freedom under the sun for virtually any point of view, except a biblical one.

• Anti-Christian feelings even reach into the funny pages. A few years before he died, Johnny Hart, creator of B.C. and The Wizard of Id comics, discovered how anti-Jesus many newspapers are. All sorts of left-wing political messages and occasionally anti-Christian jabs are allowed in the comic pages. But when Johnny Hart dared to have an overt Christian message in some of his panels of B.C., he was been bounced from several major papers, including the *Los Angeles Times*, *The Chicago Tribune*, and *The Miami Herald.* I think this subtitle from an article in *The Washington Post* shows the anti-Christian bias at work. "Everyone Loved Johnny Hart, Creator of 'B.C.'—Until He Started Drawing Cartoons About Jesus."

• When Southern Baptists mapped out a strategy to spread the gospel in the summer of 2000 in Chicago, trying to reach many non-Christians, including many Hindus, they were denounced by community leaders, even some liberal clergy, as being engaged in "hate crimes."

HOW FAR WE HAVE FALLEN

It's well-known that you can hold up Christians— evangelicals, fundamentalists, or Catholics—to ridicule, but virtually no other subgroup. In fact, it's now my opinion that liberals who oppose prejudice, racism, and bigotry of any kind actually believe that it is bigoted to not treat conservative Christians with bigotry. In other words, their understanding of tolerance demands that they be intolerant of Christians. In short, they abhor bigotry of any kind, except when it applies to conservative Christians who, they believe, deserve to be discriminated against.

How far we have fallen from the vision of the Father of Our Country who said that we would only be a happy nation if we imitate Christ. So I have two questions:

- Are we imitating Christ? No, not at present.
- Are we a happy nation? Not at present.

I remember corresponding with syndicated columnist Cal Thomas once about Christian-bashing in general, and he made an interesting remark. He actually welcomes this ridicule, provided it isn't something we bring on ourselves: "To a very large extent, I welcome 'Christian bashing' if it is for righteousness sake. I think we should look for ways to live even more righteously that the 'bashing' might increase. After all, if they hated Him, they're supposed to hate us too, right?"[193]

All of this stands in stark contrast with the vision of the founders. Some of our key founding fathers had a high view of the Bible or of Jesus Christ, even if they are now often categorized as Unitarians or the like. John Adams fits that category. Yet note what he himself said in a letter to Thomas Jefferson: "I have examined all religions, as well as my narrow sphere, my straightened means, and my busy life, would allow; and the result is that the Bible is the best Book in the world. It contains more philosophy than all the libraries I have seen; and such parts of it as I cannot reconcile to my little philosophy, I postpone for future investigation."[194]

Rev. John Witherspoon was one of the signers of the Declaration of Independence. American historian, author, and law professor John Eidsmoe notes that Witherspoon—the president of Princeton, which was thoroughly Christian at that time—is perhaps best remembered as the founding father who taught so many other founding fathers, including James Madison. John Witherspoon believed strongly that following the Bible is the key to imitating Christ. He said, "The character of a Christian must be taken from Holy Scriptures . . . the unerring standard."[195]

Even Thomas Jefferson, who sometimes held some questionable views on Christianity from an historical, orthodox perspective, once said (as noted in an earlier chapter) that Christ's morality was the best. He said, "Of all the systems of morality, ancient or modern, which have come under my observation, none appear to me so pure as that of Jesus."[196]

ACTIONS OF THE FOUNDERS OF OUR NATION

If one were to honestly examine the founders and the fledgling nation they represented, one would find abundant evidence that Christianity flourished.

Pennsylvania had a conference of representatives in 1776, separate from the national congress that met in Philadelphia. They "resolved that the members elected to the convention should be required to declare their faith in God the Father, Christ his eternal Son, the Holy Spirit, and the divine inspiration of the Scriptures."[197]

New Jersey's constitution stipulated that "No Protestant could be denied any rights or franchises on account of his religious principles; and to every person within the colony were guaranteed the right to worship God according to the dictates of his own conscience, and an immunity from all tithes or church rates, except in conformity to his own engagements."[198]

George Bancroft wrote about the people of Suffolk County, Massachusetts: "By their duty to God, their country, themselves, and posterity, they pledged the county to maintain civil and religious liberties, and to transmit them entire to future generations."[199] This statement is typical, especially from towns and counties in Puritan New England.

Christianity permeated so many of the colonists at the time of Independence. It informed their morality, as well as virtually every other aspect of their lives.

PRESIDENTS

The imitation of Christ has seen echoes in America

throughout its generations. In the 18th century, President Andrew Johnson stated about Jesus: "...we must conform our actions and our conduct to the example of Him who founded our holy religion."[200]

Theodore Roosevelt was less wordy when he declared: "Fear God; and take your own part!"[201]

President Harry S. Truman noted: "A system of morals is necessary for the welfare of any individual or any nation. The greatest system of morals in the history of the world is that set out in the Sermon on the Mount, which I would advise each one of you to study. . . ."[202]

CONCLUSION

Rather than rebelling against Jesus, we should embrace Him and emulate Him. If we imitated Him as a people, we would indeed be happier, as Washington said.

When the founders finally created and then ratified the Constitution, they were grateful to God for being able to peaceably create our nation's government. So they sent word to the new president, asking him to declare a day of thanksgiving to God for the opportunity to do this. This was all within the first year of the Constitution going into effect; therefore, it was the first year of our first president under the Constitution. Here are portions of that proclamation, dated October 3, 1789, from the then-capital of the United States, New York City:

> Whereas it is the duty of all nations to acknowledge the Providence of Almighty God, to obey His will, to be grateful for his benefits, and humbly to implore His protection and favor...Now, therefore, I do recommend and assign Thursday, the twenty-sixth day of November next, to be devoted by the People of these United States to the service of that great and glorious Being, who is the beneficent Author of all the good that was, that is, or that will be . . . that we may then unite in most humbly offering our prayers and supplications to *the great Lord and Ruler of Nations*, and beseech Him to pardon our national

and other transgressions, to enable us all, whether in public or private stations, to perform our several and relative duties properly and punctually; to render our national government a blessing to all the People, by constantly being a government of wise, just and constitutional laws, discreetly and faithfully executed and obeyed; to protect and guide all Sovereigns and Nations (especially such as have shown kindness unto us) and to bless them with good government, peace, and concord; to promote the knowledge and practice of true religion and virtue, and the increase of science among them and Us; and generally to grant unto all Mankind such a degree of temporal prosperity as He alone knows to be best.

Given under my hand, at the city of New York, the 3rd of October, in the year of our Lord one thousand seven hundred and eighty-nine.

Geo. Washington[203]

Who is the great Lord and Ruler of the Nations? Jesus, whom we shall kiss (respect, fear, pay homage to). We find this not only in Psalm 2, but in Revelation 12:5, which states of Jesus, "She gave birth to a son, a male child, who will rule all the nations with an iron scepter."

Thus, if the founding fathers had an important message for our generation, it would be: Try getting back to the imitation of Christ, if you wish for some measure of true joy.

CHAPTER SEVEN

We, the People

*Providence has given to our people
the choice of their rulers, and it is the duty, as well
as the privilege and interest of our Christian nation
to select and prefer Christians for their rulers.*[204]

John Jay,
First Chief Justice of the U.S. Supreme Court

John Jay, first Chief Justice of the U. S. Supreme Court, said, "Those who own the country ought to govern it."[205] Since there are so many Christians in this country, we ought to have a greater impact than we do. There is a great need in our day for sincere Christian men and women of principle to answer the call to serve in government.

Have you ever wondered how it is that so many people in our country claim to be Christians, yet we seem to wield such little influence in our culture? We have much less political might than our numbers. Our beliefs and morals are often held up to ridicule and attack in the media and the universities. You would think we were some small group of marginalized folk hanging on for dear life. Many of us hardly qualify as "more than conquerors." We have bought into a view of spirituality that Christ is essentially lord over our spiritual beings, but not much else.

How often have you heard the assertion that politics and religion don't mix? Or, "you can't legislate morality"? These kinds of statements are repeated so often that many people take them as gospel.

THE LORDSHIP OF CHRIST OVER ALL, INCLUDING POLITICS

Too many professing believers have a very weak view of God. Too many see Jesus as Lord of the Church or Lord of their individual lives, but not necessarily Lord over the culture—and certainly not Lord of the nations. They don't picture Christ enthroned as King, the one before whom each of us will stand. He is our maker, and His authority extends over all things. Before He gave the Great Commission in Matthew 28, He said that all authority in heaven and earth has been given to Him.

I like the way the great Dutch Christian leader and theologian, Abraham Kuyper put it. He noted that there's not one square inch in the whole universe about which Jesus can't claim, "Mine." Kuyper said of God the Son:

The Son is not to be excluded from anything. You

cannot point to any natural realm or star or comet or even descend into the depth of the earth, but it is related to Christ, not in some unimportant tangential way, but directly. There is no force in nature, no laws that control those forces that do not have their origin in that eternal Word. For this reason, it is totally false to restrict Christ to spiritual affairs and to assert that there is no point of contact between him and the natural sciences.[206]

And we would add to that the political sciences. Jesus is Lord of all.

The late D. James Kennedy had a lot to say about Christians and politics. He noted this one time:

Several years ago, I had lunch with an outstanding missionary who had been in South America for a good many years. He said to me, in effect, "How is it that on my return on rare occasions to the States, I see that there is an apparent evangelical awakening, a revival of sorts, super churches, tremendous television and radio ministries, great crusades and conferences, and thousands of people coming out to them? How is it that I still see the whole moral fiber of the country continuing to slip? Why is there still the increasing pornography, the increasing ungodliness in the laws that are passed, the unconcern for human life?"

The problem is that though there are many Christians in this country, though we can say that about 36 percent of adults claim that they have had a conversion experience, and though that number is growing, that is still a minority. It just so happens that evangelical Christians are generally not making the laws in the Senate or in the Congress; they are not the ones running our television networks; they are not the ones printing pornographic material, nor allowing the laws which permit it. Though Christianity is growing in this country, it is still far from being the controlling force.[207]

We'll read more from Dr. Kennedy subsequently.

A COMMON MISPERCEPTION

For a long time, there has been a common perception among Christians that politics and religion don't mix. Perhaps this is an outgrowth of politicians abusing Christians for their own purposes. Perhaps this is an outgrowth of trying to avoid what I call "the Medieval mistake"—using the sword to try to enforce Christian doctrine.

Mistaken "Christians" used the sword to punish heretics. This has brought nothing but dishonor to Christ. (How many times are we confronted about the Crusades or the Inquisition?) The Muslims still use violence to enforce outward conformity to their doctrines, in accordance with the Koran. But this is something the Bible does not teach.

So are we as Christians to be involved in politics? The founders certainly believed so, and the vast majority of them were Christians.

I like the way the 30th president, Calvin Coolidge, once put it: "If good men don't hold office, bad men will."[208]

Meanwhile, let me partially answer the question about whether Christians should be involved in politics by using a lengthy illustration from history. Although this anecdote is from a Christian of another country, it applies to us here in America—as well as Christians the world over.

William Wilberforce (1759-1833) was seeking guidance. He had been elected to Parliament at age 21, and at 25 had been elected to represent the largest county in all of England: Yorkshire. He then underwent a dramatic conversion to Jesus Christ. But now that he was a Christian, he felt, perhaps, he should resign his position in Parliament, because he thought it was too worldly.

He went to see John Newton who, by the way, was the author of the familiar hymns "Amazing Grace" and "How Sweet the Name of Jesus Sounds." Newton had grown up in a very rough and ready way. He was a slave trader—transporting slaves from the West coast of Africa to the markets of the Western world, until God reached out and transformed this rough and godless man into a saintly man of Christ. Newton became a minister of the Gospel.

Wilberforce went to see Newton, asking him essentially this question: "Since I'm a Christian now, and I want to serve the Lord, should I leave politics and go into the ministry?" Newton answered that maybe God could use him there in politics. Newton told Wilberforce, "The Lord has raised you up to the good of his church and for the good of the nation."[209] So Wilberforce decided not to resign his position in Parliament.

One day William Pitt, a leader in Parliament, visited Wilberforce at his country home. Pitt told him, "Wilberforce, England needs a crusader to wake her up. This slave trade is horrible business. I agree, it will be a long, hard fight, but someone must take the lead. *William, you are that man.*"[210]

Wilberforce felt that God was speaking to him, through Newton, through Pitt, and through prayer—that he should indeed fight against slavery. Slavery had an incredibly vested interest. This would not be an easy struggle.

As John Wesley was dying, he wrote a letter to encourage Wilberforce in his anti-slavery crusade. He likened the statesman to "Athanasius *contra mundum.*"[211] Athanasius was the 4th century champion of the biblical doctrine of the Trinity. Even when the whole world was against him (*contra mundum*), he was faithful. So was Wilberforce.

Wilberforce was also concerned about how he could be used by God in his age. In 1787, he wrote: "Almighty God has set before me two great objectives, the abolition of the slave trade and the reformation of morals."[212] And so he formed two societies: The Committee for the Abolition of the Slave Trade, and The Society for the Reformation of Manners, which was designed to raise the moral standards of Englishmen. (I guess this was the first Moral Majority that ever existed.) Later, he was also involved in missions and Bible societies.

William Wilberforce successfully led the crusade against slavery in the British Empire. But it took about a half century. First, he fought the slave trade; that took about a quarter century. Finally, he got all the slaves free in the British empire; that took about the same time. As he was dying in 1833 (having retired in 1825 and handed the baton to others), he received the good news that all the slaves in the empire were now freed. The efforts to free the slaves in England had a positive impact on the efforts to free the slaves in America.

Whenever Christians in modern America say we as believers should have nothing to do with politics, I always think of the shining counter-example of William Wilberforce. What if John Newton had said, "Young man, you're right. If you really want to serve Christ, get out of politics"? Yet I hear these kinds of statements today from well-meaning Christians. I think it's better to say that different people have different callings, but all of us as Christians are called to be salt and light.

FURTHER INSIGHTS FROM DR. KENNEDY

No one in our time had a better perspective on this than my long-time pastor and mentor, the late Dr. D. James Kennedy. I came to work for Coral Ridge Ministries (now Truth in Action Ministries) in 1985. (By the grace of God, I am now the employee with the longest service.)

I had the privilege of working directly with Dr. Kennedy, especially as a producer of some of his television and radio programs. Also, I had the privilege of co-writing several books with him. Dr. Kennedy was a statesman and a gentleman.

Some people accused him, falsely, of "preaching politics." In reality, Dr. Kennedy preached "the whole counsel of God." He preached what the Scriptures teach on all subjects. That teaching has implications for politics.

In one of the books Dr. Kennedy and I co-wrote, we elaborated further on the same basic theme. Christians should be involved in politics—just as they should be involved in the arts, in music, in the media, in education, in the law, in medicine, in science, and in virtually every walk of life—as long as it's not immoral. Christians should do their best to serve to the glory of God, even if it's a secular pursuit. Rev. Martin Luther King, Jr. once said, "If a man is called to be a street sweeper, he should sweep streets even as Michelangelo painted, or Beethoven composed music, or Shakespeare wrote poetry. He should sweep streets so well that all the hosts of heaven and earth will pause to say, here lived a great street sweeper who did his job well."

Here is a lengthy passage on Christians and politics from our book, *The Gates of Hell Shall Not Prevail*. Although written in 1996, everything is still relevant for today:

> Someone said to me years ago, "Do you think Christians should be involved in politics? That's dirty business." I said, "Of course not, you should leave it to the atheists; otherwise, you wouldn't have anything to complain about." Well, we have got plenty to complain about today, because that is exactly what we've done.
>
> We have been commanded by Christ to render unto Caesar the things that are Caesar's. But how do we do that? First, we should pray regularly, faithfully, and daily, for those who are in power—for our president and vice president, for our Cabinet, the Supreme Court, the Congress, the Senate, the House, and those who rule locally.
>
> Secondly, we must register to vote. A lady who works in one of our precincts said that the average turnout in her precinct is 10 percent. Furthermore, it's amazing that up until the last decade and a half, huge blocs of people in the Church were not even registered to vote. In fact, according to a study about 15 years ago, eighteen and a half million evangelical Christians were not even registered to vote. Half of those who were registered never voted, and a good number of those few who did, didn't even know what they were voting for; they were not informed. Do you realize that those eighteen and a half million people could have totally changed every election that has taken place in the last fifty years? Bill Clinton squeaked by with only 43 percent of the vote, but he still beat George [H. W.] Bush by about 4 percent.

Christians have had it in their power to change all of these things that we lament and complain and grumble about, and we just haven't done it. Providentially, we saw in the 1994 elections that this abysmal situation has begun to change significantly. We have come a long way; we still have more to go. Even though we have made progress, there is still a significant group of evangelicals not registered to vote. Some of the greatest letters I've received from my television audience are those from elderly viewers that tell me they hadn't voted for many decades, until they saw one of my broadcasts. I thank God that He's using these television programs for positive change.

The Church is like a sleeping giant that is beginning to arouse from slumber. It's not totally alert yet, but it is awake. About five years ago, author and former political liaison for President Bush, Doug Wead, once said this of the Church and politics when he was asked if politicians take evangelicals seriously: "I think they kind of treat the evangelical movement like a seven foot tall high schooler who can't play basketball. If he ever learns how to play, he's going to be awesome. In the meantime, they'll do everything they can to take advantage of his awkwardness."

Voting, for non-Christian Americans, is a privilege and a responsibility; for Christians, it is a *duty* that we should fulfill.

Third, we should become informed so we don't simply walk into voting booths and close our eyes and punch holes in cards. At election time, look for the biblically oriented candidate scorecards. They are very helpful. You should get your information from many sources. Then, get involved.

Do more than just vote. Support candidates of your choice. There are many Christians who have run for office who have lamented that they have received very little help from other Christians. Support candidates. Work for them. Run for office. I am grateful that I have people in my own congregation who have run for office and who have been elected. I hope more and more Christians will consider doing the same thing. . . .

I pointed out earlier, that there are more than 65 million adults who are born again Christians in this country. Meanwhile, homosexuals represent a very small population of this country. In fact, homosexuals (men and women) and bisexuals represent, at most, only about 2.1 percent of the U.S. adult population, according to the recent, exhaustive survey Sex in America, under the auspices of the University of Chicago. Yet with their 2.1 percent, they still have a stranglehold on the media. That's because the media concur with the homosexual agenda and they disagree with ours. However, they also would like to have a paycheck on Friday. If there were enough Christians that really were concerned, then boycotts would be devastating and could close them down or cause them to have to lay off a lot of people. They would then listen more carefully.

Ultimately, you're not going to have a Christian morality in a pagan nation where most of the people are unbelievers and where the Christians are only a minority. Christian morality can't be imposed (nor should it be) by a Christian minority upon a vast majority of non-Christians. That's not going to happen. You can do it the other way around. You can take 3 percent of the people and impose communism on a country because "political power comes out of the barrel of a gun," as Chairman Mao said, or as Hitler said in *Mein Kampf,* "What is refused to amicable methods, it is up to the fist to take." But Christians don't use machine guns or the fist. All we have is a ballot, and we're not up to 51 percent of the population. Yet.

I can think of an example or two where a Christian minority won an election but were unable to impose their agenda on a district largely uninterested in their agenda. In a local town here, some conservatives got all exercised a few years ago. They got together, they got organized. They elected a whole slate of conservative city commissioners. They went in and changed everything in that city, and they put in a lot of conservative measures. But what they simply did was to awaken the beast: when the bear (the large majority of the population) woke up, in the next election they swept them out of office.

Recently, in Jacksonville, a similar thing happened. This time it wasn't conservatives; it was Christians—Christian conservatives that got together in their local churches. They won seats on the city commission, on the school board, and so on. They put into the schools abstinence based sex education, the teaching of creation, etc. When the next election came along, they lost the majority on the school board. So now all those things are going out. You can organize and be active while the beast is asleep; but when you win the election, you're going to wake them up,and they're going to sweep you right out of their lair. What you need to do is to win more people to Christ. That way, if you have, say, 55 percent on your side, even if you do wake up the secularists, that's too bad for them.

In the case of the courts, we've seen many situations where the overwhelming majority favors a particular initiative—only to see it overturned by some liberal judge. To make a difference in that realm is a much more long term process. That's not going to happen with one election. Just suppose that 60 percent of the people in this country were conservative, born again Christians. Then you add the other conservatives in the nation, and you would have conservative Christians elected to office all over the place. They would be appointing judges, and they wouldn't be appointing ACLU type judges. They wouldn't be appointed judges like those that killed Amendment 2 (a measure that was won by a majority vote which denied homosexuals special rights in the state of Colorado).

They would be appointing judges that had Christian convictions and believed in Christian principles, such as John Jay, the first Chief Justice of the U.S. Supreme Court said. He was an outspoken evangelical. It's going to take time to replace those liberal judges who sit on the bench now. It's going to take a solid majority, not just a charismatic, Ronald Reagan who gets in for a little while and makes some positive changes, but then the liberals come back in and undo it.

The only way to have long term change in this country is through evangelism. May God empower and embolden more and more of His Church today to live up to our lofty calling. . . .

For whom should Christians vote? For those who embrace their moral, spiritual, and political values as informed by the Scripture.

Have you ever heard the point made that Christians in this Christian nation should select and prefer Christians for their rulers? That sounds like it came right from the lips of Jerry Falwell, doesn't it? That's a biased un-American radical right fringe statement if I ever heard one. At least, I am sure that is the way *The Washington Post* would describe it. But the interesting thing is, Jerry Falwell never said it. It was said by John Jay. John Jay was, of course, the first Chief Justice of the first Supreme Court of the United States. He was appointed to that august position by the Father of Our Country, George Washington, who obviously held him in the highest esteem. John Jay, with Madison and Hamilton, authored the Federalist Papers, which explained the meaning of the new Constitution and sold the states on ratifying and adopting it as the law governing the United States. Thus, Jay was one of the central Founders of America, and he said, "Providence has given to our people the choice of their rulers, and it is the duty, as well as the privilege and interest of our Christian nation to select and prefer Christians for their rulers."

A radical, far-out fringe statement. You will have to go a long way to prove that John Jay was of those things. No, this was and is a Christian nation. Thus it was established: 99.8 percent of the people, as late as 1776 professed themselves to be Protestant or Catholic Christians.

Isn't it interesting, as Dr. Reed says, that only in recent times have religious conservatives, or religious people of any kind, been viewed as trying to transform this country into something that critics do not want to admit that it always has been: namely a Christian nation.

But now we are beginning to see some tremendous signs of an awakening of evangelical Christians to their responsibilities to the culture in which they live. Political philosopher Russell Kirk put it very well when he pointed out that "culture" comes from the same root as "cult"— cult in the general sense meaning "religion," and that no culture can thrive if it is severed from the religious vision that gave it birth. That is exactly what the atheists, the secularists, and the humanists have been doing for the past forty years. They have done their very best to sever this culture from the religious vision which was the vision of the Pilgrims, the vision of the Puritans, the vision of the Founders of this country.

I believe a time is coming and soon will be upon us that we shall return to that vision of the Founders of America. Christians should be encouraged. We should be encouraged to realize that we are not losing, and defeated, and discouraged, and marginalized. Rather, just the opposite is true. We need to realize we can make a difference—we can make a determinative difference in the direction of this country. We have had 40 years of secular humanistic principles imposed upon this country, which have delivered chaos and corruption. I think

American Christians are waking up to say, "Enough is enough. We are going to change America back again to what it once was."

How can this be accomplished? By fulfilling the Great Commission. By obeying the Cultural Mandate, which means to take all the potentialities of this world—in other words, all of its spheres and institutions—and bring them all to the glory of God. By being both light and salt. By rendering unto God the things that are God's and unto Caesar the things that are Caesar's.

C. S. Lewis, the great author from Oxford and Cambridge, put it so interestingly: "He who converts his neighbour has performed the most practical Christian political act of all." I couldn't agree with him more. But second to that is that we become involved in our culture and regraft it into that vision which gave it its original life.

We need to be able to discern the signs of the times, and our politicians and cultural elites had better discern them, because. . . the Christians are coming.

So from the beginning,
the fight we were winning.
Thou, Lord, be at our side.
All glory be Thine.[213]

An interesting comment on rendering unto Caesar the things that are Caesar's comes from Gary DeMar. He points out that for us as modern Americans, our "Caesar" is the Constitution, which allows for its citizens to address grievances. Therefore, in rendering unto Caesar, we have every opportunity—thanks to the Christian influence in the founding of the Constitution—for us to petition our government if things are going astray.

ARE CHRISTIANS WAKING UP?

It seems that many Christians have begun to get involved in politics. They are treated like Johnnies-come-lately. They are often treated as if they are from Mars—not as if they represent the views of the vast majority of the founders. It's great to see strong Christians (in some cases, on both sides of the aisle), trying to faithfully live for Christ as public servants in politics. As of this writing, I can think of a number of strong professing Christians who are active in politics. They are often movers and shakers in Washington, D.C. and on the campaign trail. They are also lightning rods for virtually every accusation the forces of secularism can throw their way. What counts is their faithfulness to Christian principles, while serving their constituencies faithfully. The number of Christians in politics of late has been encouraging.

We still have a great need for better judges. How many evangelical judges can you think of? The only one I can think of is former Chief Justice Roy S. Moore of Alabama. The problem is that he no longer serves on the bench. May the Lord raise him up and others like him to make a major difference on the courts.

The 2010 mid-term election was significant in many ways. One of those ways is that it showed that the value voters still matter. Those who care about abortion. Those who favor traditional marriage. Those who believe in fiscal responsibility.

By his own admission, President Obama got a "shellacking" in the vote. And I might add it was well-deserved. There's too much of an elitist attitude in Washington, D.C., these days.

Evangelicals and conservative Catholics swung that election. They showed up. In fact, they showed up in record numbers. According to a survey by the Faith and Freedom Coalition, the "largest single constituency" going to the polls during that election was "self-identified evangelicals." They represented 29% of those who voted. How did they vote? 78% voted conservatively.

In addition to evangelical voters, 12% of those who voted in the mid-term were Catholics who frequently attend church. They voted 58% for professed conservatives versus 40% for professed liberal candidates. As to Catholics overall (church-goers and non-church-goers mixed together), they voted this time 53% for the Republican candidates and 45% for the Democratic ones. What's fascinating about the Catholic vote is the change from just two years before. Between 2008 and 2010, there was an astounding 18 point shift, from liberal to conservative.

Ralph Reed, who was the president of the Christian Coalition in its heyday in the 1990s, founded and leads the Faith and Freedom Coalition. He said of the 2010 vote, "People of faith turned out in the highest numbers in a midterm election we have ever seen, and they made an invaluable contribution to the historic results."

Issues like abortion, traditional marriage, and fiscal responsibility were key ones.

Steven Ertelt, who runs the Life News website, a pro-life clearing house on the abortion issue, said on the day after the election, "Look no further than the health care reform bill that allows for taxpayer funding of abortions as the reason why so many pro-life candidates won elections to federal and state offices on Tuesday."

One study on the issue of abortion found that abortion was important to 30% of those who voted. This, according to results from the conservative group, the polling company™ inc. Pro-life candidates enjoyed a 3-to-1 advantage over their abortion-choice counterparts, all things being equal. Here's the breakdown: 22% of all voters voted pro-life. 8% of all voters voted abortion-choice.

Traditional marriage also fared well in the 2010 election. For example, three of the Supreme Court justices of Iowa were voted out. Why? Because before the election, they found "the right" for same-sex couples to marry in the Iowa constitution. These three justices were specifically targeted by the voters for trying to force same-sex marriage on the state by judicial fiat. Now, thankfully, they're out of a job.

Writer Jim Jewel summed up the values voters' contributions to the 2010 election this way: "Exit polling showed that not only did the Republican wildfire spread throughout the country but that the coalition of white evangelicals and Catholics that powered prior conservative success (before the youthful senator from Illinois split the alliance) fueled the 2010 inferno."

Obviously, the Tea Party movement played an important role in the 2010 election. Just two years ago, the only reference to a Tea Party rally was in the history books—in reference to the Boston Tea Party. Jump ahead to 2009 and 2010, where we see a new Tea Party movement impacting the outcome of the national election. Election-wise, the Tea Party movement won some and lost some. The pundits sneer at it as if it's a net negative. Yet the amazing thing is that such a new movement, not even two years old, would have such amazing results as to propel a few candidates into prominent, national office. Some 52% of Tea Party members are self-identified evangelicals.

Thus, the values voters made a huge difference in that election. Ralph Reed said there's a lesson for all politicians from the 2010 mid-term election: "...those who ignore or disregard social conservative voters and their issues do so at their own peril."

THOUGHTS FROM SOME OF OUR PRESIDENTS

Nature abhors a vacuum. If we as Christians are not involved in politics, then ungodly men and women will be. Look at what Abraham Lincoln said: "Our government rests in public opinion. Whoever can change public opinion can change the government practically just so much."[214] He also noted this—a statement that I think about in light of the ACLU and other secularists trying to rob us of our liberties and our rich Christian heritage: "A majority held in restraint by constitutional checks and limitations, and always changing easily with deliberate changes of popular opinions and sentiments, is the only true sovereign of a free republic."[215]

After Lincoln, our 17th President, Andrew Johnson, said what we have been saying here repeatedly, that our rights are God-given. Said Johnson: "This is the peoples' Government; they received it as a legacy from Heaven, and they must defend it and preserve it."[216]

Our 26th president was Theodore Roosevelt. He reminds

us of the arduous task government is for we the people: "The noblest of all forms of government is self-government; but it is also the most difficult."[217]

CONCLUSION

I close with further words of President Theodore Roosevelt, whom I quoted earlier— "Fear God, and take your part!" He also said this about the American political system: "The government is us; we are the government, you and I." [218] Finally, Roosevelt gave a warning we should all heed—perhaps Christians especially: "If people cannot rule themselves, then they are not fit for free government, and all talk about democracy is a sham."[219]

CHAPTER EIGHT

Limited Government

If men were angels,
no government would be necessary.[220]

James Madison

James Madison played an important role in the writing of our Constitution. He noted that since men are not angels, government is necessary. But men are not angels, and since government is run by men, we need protection from the government. Belief in the sinfulness of man can be seen in the details of the Constitution with its strict separation of powers.

The Bible is very clear. It does not teach that we are perfect, but rather that we are sinful. Jesus said, "If you then, who are evil..." (Matthew 7:11 ESV).

Just look at this small collection of other verses:

- "None is righteous, no, not one" (Romans 3:10 ESV).
- "...for all have sinned and fall short of the glory of God" (Romans 3:23 ESV).
- "The heart is deceitful above all things, and desperately sick; who can understand it?" (Jeremiah 17:9 ESV).

Man is evil. Therefore, power must be separated.

I honestly believe that one would be hard-pressed to find a single example of any of the founders of America believing that man was basically good. This is not cynical. It's just the reality and has led to the most prosperous forms of government—and economics too.

Like the other founders, Thomas Jefferson said that power should be divided for everybody's sake: "The way to have good and safe government is not to trust it all to one, but to divide it among the many. . . ."[221]

JOHN WITHERSPOON

As we have seen, Rev. John Witherspoon was president of what is now Princeton from 1768 to 1794, and served as a delegate from New Jersey in the third Continental Congress—the one that gave us the Declaration of Independence. John Adams once heard him as a preacher and said of Witherspoon: "Heard Dr. Witherspoon all Day. A clear, sensible, Preacher."[222]

Witherspoon taught what Christians have taught from

the beginning: that man's basic nature is fallen. Christ came to redeem sinners who cannot save themselves. Witherspoon wrote:

> The corruption of our nature . . . is the foundation-stone of the doctrine of redemption. Nothing can be more absolutely necessary to true religion, than a clear conviction of the sinfulness of our nature and state. . . .
>
> Men of lax and corrupt principles take great delight in speaking to the praise of human nature, and extolling its dignity, without distinguishing what it was at its first creation, from what it is in its present fallen state. But I appeal from these visionaries' reasonings to the history of all ages, and the inflexible testimony of daily experience....
>
> The evil of sin appears from every page of the sacred oracles....The history of the world is little else than the history of human guilt. . . .
>
> Nothing is more plain from scripture, or better supported by daily experience, than that man by nature is in fact incapable of recovery without the power of God specially interposed.[223]

Witherspoon, in particular, and Christian theology, in general, teach that at the beginning of creation, human nature was good. When God created us humans, He pronounced His creation as "very good." It is the fall that corrupts us, and it is Christ that begins—and will finish—the process of restoration.

A fascinating aspect of Witherspoon is the impact he had on other founders. As the head of Princeton, this native of Scotland had great influence on a number of our founding fathers. The most notable example was James Madison, who was active at the Constitutional convention and even took notes of the proceedings.

John Eidsmoe, author of the classic book, *Christianity and the Constitution,* observes that John Witherspoon's strong Presbyterian theology strongly influenced Madison's political science.[224]

In a statement reflecting Witherspoon—and really, Calvinism, and more specifically, the Scriptures—Madison said, "All men having power ought to be distrusted."[225]

THE BACKGROUND OF THE CONSTITUTION

After the Constitution was written in 1787, it had to be ratified by a majority of the states (but not all of them unanimously). The original constitution of these United States was the Articles of Confederation, written in 1777 and ratified in 1781, which, like all of America's key documents, mentions God in one way or the other. (The Constitution itself was signed "in the year of our Lord"). Here's one portion of the Articles of Confederation:

> And whereas it has pleased the Great Governor of the World to incline the hearts of the Legislatures we respectively represent in Congress, to approve of, and to authorize us to ratify the said Articles of Confederation and perpetual union.[226]

Although it was our first working constitution, it didn't work. One great flaw was that it required that all the states (at that time, of course, being only thirteen) had to agree before anything could get passed.

Because the Articles of Confederation was *not* working, fifty-five delegates from twelve of the thirteen states met in the summer of 1787 to revise them. (Rhode Island didn't even bother to send a delegate.) This is what we call the Constitutional Convention.

Soon they decided to start all over again, and the Constitution was born—after much struggle. By the time it was signed on September 17, 1787, 224 years from the very day I write this sentence, only thirty-nine of the delegates were left to affix their signatures. Many of the delegates had already left and didn't bother to come back.

THE FEDERALIST PAPERS

Once written and signed, the drafters of the Constitution

had to get it ratified. This was a tough sales job. New York was a key swing state. So three of our most brilliant founding fathers, Alexander Hamilton, James Madison, and John Jay, wrote letters under an assumed name (Publius) to convince the men of New York to accept the new charter.

As best as scholars can tell, Hamilton wrote 51, Madison, 26, and John Jay 5.[227]

Those brilliant letters are collectively known as *The Federalist Papers,* and they are among the finest political arguments America has ever produced. Clearly, they reflect a biblical worldview, including the sinfulness of man.

Madison wrote in *Federalist 10:* "It is in vain to say that enlightened statesmen will be able to adjust these clashing interests and render them all subservient to the public good. Enlightened statesmen will not always be at the helm."[228]

Then in *Federalist 47,* Madison spelled out how governmental power had to be divvied up between competing forces, lest one group lord it over another: "The accumulation of all powers, legislative, executive, and judiciary, in the same hands, whether of one, a few, or many, and whether hereditary, self-appointed, or elective, may justly be pronounced the very definition of tyranny."[229]

And so as John Eidsmoe points out: "One thing is certain, the Christian religion, particularly Rev. Witherspoon's Calvinism, influenced Madison's view of law and government."[230] Eidsmoe writes, "And although Witherspoon derived the concept of separation of powers from other sources, such as Montesquieu, checks and balances seem to have been his own unique contribution to the foundation of U.S. Government."[231]

Perhaps Madison's most famous statement on the sinfulness of man and political power comes from *Federalist* 51:

> But what is government itself, but the greatest of all
> reflections on human nature? If men were angels,
> no government would be necessary. If angels were
> to govern men, neither external nor internal
> controls on government would be necessary. In
> framing a government which is to be administered

by men over men, the great difficulty lies in this: you must first enable the government to control the governed; and in the next place oblige it to control itself. A dependence on the people is, no doubt, the primary control on the government; but experience has taught mankind the necessity of auxiliary precautions.[232]

This is very rich. Madison is saying that not only do we need government to protect us from our fellow human beings, who are not angels, but we need to be protected from the government, which is run by human beings, who are not angels.

Federalist 55 was written either by Hamilton or Madison; scholars are not sure which. In any event, there is a ringing declaration of man's sinfulness and how that relates to government:

As there is a degree of depravity in mankind which requires a certain degree of circumspection and distrust, so there are other qualities in human nature which justify a certain portion of esteem and confidence. Republican government presupposes the existence of these qualities in a higher degree than any other form. Were the pictures which have been drawn by the political jealousy of some among us faithful likenesses of the human character, the inference would be, that there is not sufficient virtue among men for self-government; and that nothing less than the chains of despotism can restrain them from destroying and devouring one another.[233]

Recognition of the reality of man's sinful nature played a key role in the writing and selling of the U.S. Constitution. It also explains the success of the Constitution, overall.

Alexander Hamilton wrote in *Federalist* 6: "Is it not time to awake from the deceitful dream of a golden age and to adopt as a practical maxim for the direction of our political conduct that we, as well as the other inhabitants of the globe, are yet remote from the happy empire of perfect wisdom and perfect virtue?"[234] Hamilton added in *Federalist* 15, "Why has government been instituted at all? Because the passions of men will not conform to the dictates of reason and justice without constraint."[235]

THE FOUNDERS ON MAN'S FALLEN STATE

Consider these statements from some founders about our sinful nature:

- Ben Franklin: "There is scarce a king in a hundred who would not, if he could, follow the example of Pharaoh, get first all the peoples' money, then all their lands and then make them and their children servants forever."[236]
- Alexander Hamilton: "Til the millennium comes, in spite of all our boasted light and purification, hypocrisy and treachery will continue to be the most successful commodities in the political market."[237]
- Author Catherine Drinker Bowen writes of our second president, a key founding father: "John Adams saw every man in power as 'a ravenous beast of prey,' who must be checked, controlled, balanced by other governmental powers."[238]
- As a practicing, faithful 18th century Anglican, George Washington affirmed the doctrines of his Church, which taught that we are all sinners and Christ came to save sinners. He implied that since government was force, and since humans can misuse force, government should be limited. Things break down when man is left to his own sinful devices. Said Washington: "Mankind when left to themselves, are unfit for their own Government."[239]

The founders were tired of the abuse of force, as they had been experiencing at the hands of King George, much of Parliament, and many of the British appointees in the colonies.

NOT ALL AGREE

Anthropology is the study of man. A nation is much better off if it agrees with the Bible's anthropology than modern humanistic notions about the nature of man. I find it interesting that we enjoy the great freedoms we have in America because the founders, recognizing the sinfulness of man, separated government's powers so that no one group could lord it over others. Meanwhile, the modern humanist has a high view of man's basic nature, and the governments he controls always end up taking away freedom.

The Soviets built their system of government on an atheistic, Marxist base—on the notion that man is basically good, but corrupted by capitalism and religion. So the new Soviet man (and woman) was to be free from religious superstitions and from the curse of selfishness as found in capitalism with its emphasis on private property.

Who created a better system? The Communists or America's founders? The answer is obvious.

But today many of our elites believe that man is basically good, and they do what they can to try and agitate for more redistribution of wealth, putting liberty at risk as a result.

Think of the ACLU as an example. I can think of no organization that has done more to try to reshape America, not in the image of our nation's founders, but in the image of the founders of the failed Soviet Union, than the American Civil Liberties Union. Roger Baldwin, the founder and long-time head of the ACLU, said in his official biography:

> I believe, generally speaking, that the human race is fundamentally good in the sense that people want to get along with each other. And if you think that people are good and can live by the Golden Rule, and you have faith in them as I do, then you believe that social relations are perfectible. Therefore, you can have a government that works without conflict and a society that is not bent on self-destruction. Now when you cast it on a world scale—you believe in the same thing—the capacity of people of all

nations and colors and races to get along with each other and to create a world order.[240]

Ideas have consequences.

For a century and more, the world has been plagued by Karl Marx's philosophy and more than 100 million have died as a result. Karl Marx believed that man was good, but the system (capitalism) was bad.

In Whittaker Chamber's book, *Witness,* you can see clearly that he and other Communists believed that man was good, but the system was bad and needed changing. (Chambers later rejected Communism and embraced Christ.) The 1960s radicals believed in man's goodness. They never left the university. Now they just have tenure and have taken over academia, where this mistaken view prevails.

GOOD OR BAD?

D. James Kennedy and I wrote about the importance of a biblical anthropology for good government. The following is an excerpt from our book, *Lord of All,* which is essentially a world-view primer:

> The United States was clearly based upon a religious, specifically Christian concept, whereas, for example, Nazism and communism are very clearly based upon an anti-religious concept of materialistic humanism and anti-Christian and anti-God sentiments. All of these non-theistic views say that man is basically good. What did Karl Marx say? Essentially, that once the workers achieve their revolution and set up the "worker's paradise," the government will wither away because government will be proven unnecessary. Try telling a Cuban today or a Russian thirty years ago he was living in "paradise." Marx got it wrong at the foundation of his theory because he had a false view of anthropology.
>
> Man's nature—are we perfectible in our own strength, or are we corrupt? This is a theological concept, and it is vitally important in the outworking

of one's view of politics. It is vitally important when you walk into a voting booth to cast your ballot.

In a discussion of the fact that all humanist views of government declare that man is good, the philosopher Dr. Gordon Clark says that socialists of all stripes are very inconsistent at this point. Psychologically, they declare that man is good, but when they pass from psychology to politics, it turns out that only poor men are good, and that somehow the rich have become evil. Then, if this is not inconsistent enough, in their demands for more and more governmental regulation, they clearly imply that not merely are poor people good, but politicians are even better. Since they apparently are immune from all temptation and evil and the profit motive, they should be trusted to regulate all of our daily affairs—an obvious contradiction.

In fact, it is vitally important to understand that in all humanistic and socialistic concepts of government, it would seem that wealth corrupts, but power does not. Remember that, because all of history would rise up with one voice to proclaim that thought is a lie. It is axiomatic in history, as Lord Acton (1834-1902) pointed out, that "power corrupts, and absolute power corrupts absolutely." Notice how often you will be faced with a decision that deals with this very question—the humanistic concept that wealth corrupts, but power does not.

The founders of America, because of their clear understanding of the teachings of Christ, knew that man basically is evil; therefore, they designed the form of government that took into consideration their religious understanding of the nature of man as being evil. Jesus said, "If you then, who are evil" (Matthew 7:11 ESV).[241]

CONCLUSION

The consequence for political stability of the view of man incorporated into a nation's charter is illustrated by the contrast between the American and French revolutions, as David Gibbs,

Jr., points out in a book he and I co-authored, *One Nation Under God: Ten Things Every Christian Should Know About the Founding of America*:

> By believing in man's sinfulness, the founders gave us a much more secure government than any kind based on the assumption that man is basically good. Author and speaker William J. Federer points out an interesting contrast: the founders of the United States with the French Revolutionaries. The founders of America began with the assumption that man is basically evil and that we must protect ourselves even from those who run the government. The founders were well acquainted with verses like Jeremiah 17:9, which declares, "The heart is deceitful above all things, and desperately wicked: who can know it?" In contrast, the French began with the teaching of Jean Jacques Rousseau, who believed that man was basically good, once the people could remake the government in their image. But Rousseau's idealistic, utopian, unrealistic, unbiblical view of man led to a relentless bloodbath in the French Revolution. France has gone through a dozen new overhauls in their governmental system and a number of new constitutions, while in the same time, the United States is still ruled by the one and only Constitution.[242]

The founders would not approve of any modern scheme that puts power into the hands of just a few. For the sake of our nation's future, we need to recapture a biblical anthropology and its implications to government.

CHAPTER NINE

Courage

If your cause is just,
if your principles are pure, and if your
conduct is prudent, you need not fear the
multitude of opposing hosts.[243]

Declaration Signer
Rev. John Witherspoon

Declaration signer Rev. John Witherspoon said that if our cause is correct, we should trust in God and not live in fear, despite what odds we may face. Witherspoon advocated that we fear God, but not man. We need courage and trust in the Lord for such trying times, even when many men oppose us.

ONE OF WITHERSPOON'S SERMONS

One of the common practices during the American War for Independence was to call for national days of fasting and prayer. This was done frequently at the local level and at the national level. For example, the Continental Congress called for a national day of fasting and prayer on May 17, 1775. New Jersey had delegated John Witherspoon to be one of their representatives in Congress. Furthermore, the president of Princeton was called upon to preach the sermon for that day. His topic was "The Dominion of Providence over the Affairs of Men." In that message, Rev. Witherspoon made the following observations:

> . . . let us guard against the dangerous error of trusting in, or boasting of, an arm of flesh. . . . If your cause is just, if your principles are pure, and if your conduct is prudent, you need not fear the multitude of opposing hosts.
>
> What follows from this? That he is the best friend to American liberty, who is most sincere and active in promoting true and undefiled religion, and who sets himself with the greatest firmness to bear down profanity and immorality of every kind.
>
> Whoever is an avowed enemy of God, I scruple not to call him an enemy of his country.[244]

Nothing politically correct here. If you're an enemy of God, then as far as Witherspoon was concerned, you're an enemy of America—allowing for the fact that these words were said during war time.

"AN ELOQUENT SCOTTISH MINISTER"

We have spoken a lot about Witherspoon in this book. He played an important role in the founding of America, and was a strongly committed Christian. Tragically, he is virtually unknown by millions of Americans today. George Bancroft, author of a six-volume history of the United States, writes this about John Witherspoon:

> The provincial congress of New Jersey, which came fresh from the people with ample powers and organized itself in the evening of the eleventh of June, was opened with prayer by John Witherspoon, an eloquent Scottish minister of great ability, learning, and liberality; ready to dash into pieces all images of false gods. Born near Edinburgh, trained up at its university, in 1768 he removed to Princeton, to become the successor of Jonathan Edwards, Davis, and Finley, as president of its college. A combatant of skepticism and the narrow philosophy of the materialists, he was deputed by Somerset county to take part in applying his noble theories to the construction of a civil government.[245]

With British troops and ships pouring into the Atlantic coast, Americans needed courage. For the most part, they sought the Lord for that courage. The Americans—including Congress—called again for national days of fasting and prayer.

George Bancroft notes that during the war, "Eloquent chaplains kept alive the custom of daily prayer and weekly sermons."[246]

Chaplain Emerson declared: "There are many things amiss in this camp . . . yet, upon the whole, God is in the midst of us."[247]

Nathanael Greene said: "Fight or be slaves is the American motto."[248]

Bancroft reminds us what the colonists were up against: "Edmund Burke did not believe that the colonies, left to themselves, could offer any effective resistance to the whole power of England and its allies."[249] This makes sense. Here we had a rag-tag group of farmers facing the strongest nation on earth. They needed courage.

WASHINGTON

Their first key military leader was a man of deep Christian faith and a study in courage. Bancroft says this of George Washington: "No one knew better than the commander-in-chief the exceedingly discouraging aspect of military affairs; but his serene and unfaltering courage in this hour was a support to congress."[250]

Washington believed that while peace is to be preferred to war, the best way to prevent war is "peace through strength." He once noted: "There is nothing so likely to produce peace as to be well prepared to meet an enemy."[251]

SAMUEL ADAMS

There is no man more responsible for the United States coming into being than Samuel Adams, a man of great faith in Christ and a man of great courage. Bancroft notes of Sam Adams (a second cousin of John Adams): ". . . no one man had done so much to bring about independence as the elder Adams. . . ."[252]

According to Bancroft, Sam Adams "urged his friends to study the art of war, and organize resistance. 'I would advise,' said he, 'persisting in our struggle, though it were revealed from heaven that nine hundred and ninety-nine were to perish, and only one of a thousand to survive and retain his liberty.'"[253]

"Call me an enthusiast," said Samuel Adams, "[T]his union among the colonies and warmth of affection can be attributed to nothing less than the agency of the Supreme Being. If we believe that he superintends and directs the affairs of empires, we have reason to expect the restoration and establishment of the public liberties."[254]

Bancroft commented: "The congress of Massachusetts, though destitute of munitions of war, armed vessels, military stores, and money, had confidence that a small people, resolute in its convictions outweighs an empire. On the return of Samuel Adams, they adopted all the recommendations of the continental congress. They established a secret correspondence with Canada. They entreated the ministers of the gospel in their colony 'to assist in avoiding that dreadful slavery with which all were now threatened.' . . . With such words they adjourned, to keep the annual Thanksgiving which they themselves had appointed, finding occasion in their distress to rejoice at 'the smiles of Divine Providence on the union in their own province and throughout the continent.'"[255]

COURAGEOUS STEPS TOWARD INDEPENDENCE

To act as a free people was a risky venture at this time. In April 1776, Charleston, South Carolina, held its first court session, independent of Great Britain. At the time the court was first opened, the chief justice declared, "The Almighty created America to be independent of Britain; to refuse our labors in this divine work is to refuse to be a great, a free, a pious, and a happy people!"[256]

During the third Continental Congress, before the Declaration of Independence was actually written and adopted in 1776, John Dickinson from Pennsylvania hesitated to make such a declaration. "No instance is recollected of a people, without a battle fought or an ally gained, abrogating forever their connection with a warlike commercial empire. It might unite the different parties in Great Britain against us, and it might create disunion among ourselves."[257]

Bancroft describes the scene in which the president of Princeton helped carry the day: "Before the end of the debate rose Witherspoon of New Jersey. In a short speech he remarked that though he had not heard all the discussion in that body, yet he had not wanted ample sources of information; and that, in his judgment, the country was not only ripe for independence, but was in danger of becoming rotten for want of it, if its declaration were longer delayed."[258]

BRITAIN'S HIRING OF SOLDIERS

After the early battles—Lexington, Concord, Bunker Hill, and a battle in the harbor near Charleston, South Carolina—it became apparent to the British that it might not be as easy as first thought to bring the Americans into submission. There weren't enough British troops available to fully put down the rebellion in America. So King George looked eastward, initially to Russia, as a source for potential troops. Catherine the Great was in his debt, but she refused his request for troops.

The king also looked to Holland, but they too turned him down. Here is a paraphrase of the reply of Baron van der Capellan tot den Pol, a noble from the Netherlands, to the King of England's request for troops: "Why should a nation of men, who have borne the title of rebels and freed themselves from oppression by their swords, employ their troops in crushing the Americans, who yet are worthy of the esteem of the whole world as defending with moderation and with intrepidity the rights which God and not the British legislature has given them as men!" Thus, Holland said no, as did Russia.

Only with George III's relative from the House of Hanover, Frederick II, did he have any success. So England was able to recruit some Hessians from Germany. It was a dishonorable move for Frederick, observes Bancroft: "From avarice he sold the flesh of his own people while they were yet alive, depriving many of them existence and himself of honor." Frederick II may have been a strong leader and a military genius, but his greed was inherent in his philosophy of leadership: "Take what you can; you are never wrong unless you are obliged to give it back." Bancroft says of the Hessians: "Yet very many of them went willingly, having been made to believe that in America they would have free license to plunder and to indulge their passions."[259]

In the Declaration of Independence, one of the several complaints the Americans levied against the king was his use of foreign mercenaries. Talking about the King of England, Jefferson charged, "He is at this time transporting large armies of foreign mercenaries to complete the works of death, desolation and tyranny, already begun with circumstances of Cruelty & perfidy scarcely paralleled in the most barbarous ages, and totally unworthy the Head of a civilized nation."[260]

JOHN ADAMS'S OBSERVATION

England hired foreign mercenaries in part because many at home did not agree with the whole venture. The unpopularity of the war among those in Mother England was not lost on the colonists. In 1775 John Adams pointed out, "If Great Britain were united, she could subdue a country a thousand leagues off. But Great Britain is not united against us. Millions in England and Scotland think it unrighteous, impolitic, and ruinous to make war upon us; and a minister, though he may have a marble heart, will proceed with a desponding spirit."[261]

Adams went on to show how the Bible and natural law opposed the British oppression of Americans:

> I would ask by what law the parliament has authority over America? By the law in the Old and New Testament it has none; by the law of nature and nations it has none; by the common law of England it has none; by statute law it has none; the declaratory act of 1766 was made without our consent by a parliament which had no authority beyond the four seas. . . .
>
> The two characteristics of this people, religion and humanity, are strongly marked in all their proceedings. We are not exciting a rebellion. Resistance by arms against usurpation and lawless violence is not rebellion by the law of God or the land. Resistance to lawful authority makes rebellion.[262]

In short, the Americans were resisting unlawful authority and drawing upon God for the courage to do so.

The Bible teaches submission to lawful authority. It also teaches that, on rare occasions, there is a time and a place for civil disobedience, especially when the proclamation of the Gospel is at stake. If the early Church had obeyed first the Jewish authorities and then the Roman authorities in all things, there never would have been a Church, because for the first three hundred years, the Church existed illegally. This teaching of civil disobedience should not be taken out of context or abused. God is the one who set the government over us, and we are to obey the civil rulers and to pray for them. Thankfully, because of the Christian faith, we in America can petition our government for change. We can peacefully and lawfully vote out of office those who abuse their lawful authority. The founders of America did not have it so easy. Their resistance to unlawful political authority led to the shedding of blood.

PATRICK HENRY

A great example of courage in the American push for Independence can be seen in the example of Patrick Henry, another strong Christian. He once said, "The Bible is worth all other books which have ever been printed."[263]

It has been said that if Samuel Adams was the pen of the Independence (in some of his writings), then Patrick Henry was its tongue.

Henry was elected to the first Continental Congress in 1774. According to historian George Bancroft, when Patrick Henry left for the Continental Congress, there was a great celebration: "Amid salutes and huzzas, a volunteer guard accompanies him to the Maryland side of the Potomac, where, as they said farewell, they invoked God's blessing on the champion of their 'dearest rights and liberties.'"[264]

He was also elected to the Second Virginia Convention in 1775. This convention was held in St. John's Church in Richmond. It was here on March 23, 1775, that Patrick Henry gave a stirring call to arms, including the line that made him famous, "Give me liberty or give me death." Henry's classic speech was clearly one of the most memorable in the history of the United States

The context of Patrick Henry's stirring speech was that he was responding to some speeches before him against preparing for war. The naysayers weren't necessarily opposed in theory to fighting the British, but rather they were concerned about the practical matters, such as the power and might of the English army vs. the lack of preparedness of the ragtag, largely disunited colonists. Here is George Bancroft's summary of what they said in the House of Burgesses on that day:

> Are we ready for war? . . . Where are our stores, our soldiers, our generals, our money? We are defenseless; yet we talk of war against one of the most formidable nations in the world. It will be time enough to resort to measures of despair when every well-founded hope has vanished."[265]

PATRICK HENRY'S SPEECH

On that day, March 23, 1775, Patrick Henry responded with his famous words. To read this speech is to enter the presence of greatness. Here is courage, with faith in God, firmly on display for all to see. Because it's so rich, here it is in fullness:

> No man thinks more highly than I do of the patriotism, as well as abilities, of the very worthy gentlemen who have just addressed the House. But different men often see the same subject in different lights; and, therefore, I hope that it will not be thought disrespectful to those gentlemen, if, entertaining as I do opinions of a character very opposite to theirs, I shall speak forth my sentiments freely and without reserve.
>
> This is no time for ceremony. The question before the House is one of awful moment to this country. For my own part I consider it as nothing less than a question of freedom or slavery; and in proportion to the magnitude of the subject ought to be the freedom of the debate. It is only in this way that we can hope to arrive at truth, and fulfill the great responsibility which we hold to God and our country. Should I keep back my opinions at such a time, through fear of giving offense, I

should consider myself as guilty of treason towards my country and of an act of disloyalty towards the majesty of heaven, which I revere above all earthly kings.

Mr. President, it is natural to man to indulge in the illusions of hope. We are apt to shut our eyes against a painful truth, and listen to the song of that siren, till she transforms us into beasts. Is this the part of wise men, engaged in a great and arduous struggle for liberty? Are we disposed to be of the number of those who, having eyes, see not, and having ears, hear not, the things which so nearly concern their temporal salvation?

For my part, whatever anguish of spirit it may cost, I am willing to know the whole truth—to know the worst and to provide for it. I have but one lamp by which my feet are guided; and that is the lamp of experience. I know of no way of judging of the future but by the past. And judging by the past, I wish to know what there has been in the conduct of the British ministry for the last ten years, to justify those hopes with which gentlemen have been pleased to solace themselves and the House?

Is it that insidious smile with which our petition has been lately received? Trust it not, sir; it will prove a snare to your feet. Suffer not yourselves to be betrayed with a kiss. Ask yourselves how this gracious reception of our petition comports with these warlike preparations which cover our waters and darken our land. Are fleets and armies necessary to a work of love and reconciliation? Have we shown ourselves so unwilling to be reconciled that force must be called in to win back our love? Let us not deceive ourselves, sir. These are the implements of war and subjugation—the last arguments to which kings resort. I ask gentlemen, sir, what means this martial array, if its purpose be not to force us to submission? Can gentlemen assign any other possible motives for it? Has Great Britain any enemy, in this quarter of the world, to call for all this accumulation of navies and armies?

No, sir, she has none. They are meant for us; they can be meant for no other. They are sent over to bind and rivet upon us those chains which the British ministry have been so long forging. And what have we to oppose to them? Shall we try argument? Sir, we have been trying that for the last ten years. Have we anything new to offer on the subject? Nothing.

We have held the subject up in every light of which it is capable; but it has been all in vain. Shall we resort to entreaty and humble supplication? What terms shall we find which have not been already exhausted? Let us not, I beseech you, sir, deceive ourselves longer.

Sir, we have done everything that could be done to avert the storm which is now coming on. We have petitioned; we have remonstrated; we have supplicated; we have prostrated ourselves before the throne, and have implored its interposition to arrest the tyrannical hands of the ministry and Parliament.

Our petitions have been slighted; our remonstrances have produced additional violence and insult; our supplications have been disregarded; and we have been spurned, with contempt, from the foot of the throne. In vain, after these things, may we indulge the fond hope of peace and reconciliation. There is no longer any room for hope.

If we wish to be free—if we mean to preserve inviolate those inestimable privileges for which we have been so long contending—if we mean not basely to abandon the noble struggle in which we have been so long engaged, and which we have pledged ourselves never to abandon until the glorious object of our contest shall be obtained, we must fight! I repeat it, sir, we must fight! An appeal to arms and to the God of Hosts is all that is left us!

They tell us, sir, that we are weak—unable to cope with so formidable an adversary. But when shall we be stronger? Will it be the next week, or the next year? Will it be when we are totally disarmed, and when a British guard shall be stationed in every house? Shall we gather strength by irresolution and inaction? Shall we acquire the means of effectual resistance, by lying supinely on our backs, and hugging the delusive phantom of hope, until our enemies shall have bound us hand and foot?

Sir, we are not weak, if we make a proper use of the means which the God of nature hath placed in our power. Three millions of people, armed in the holy cause of liberty, and in such a country as that which we possess, are invincible by any force which our enemy can send against us. Besides, sir, we shall not fight our battles alone. There is a just God who presides over the destinies of nations, and who will raise up friends to fight our battles for us.

The battle, sir, is not to the strong alone; it is to the vigilant, the active, the brave. Besides, sir, we have no election. If we were base enough to desire it, it is now too late to retire from the contest. There is no retreat but in submission and slavery! Our chains are forged! Their clanking may be heard on the plains of Boston! The war is inevitable—and let it come! I repeat it, sir, let it come!

It is in vain, sir, to extenuate the matter. Gentlemen may cry, "Peace! Peace!" —but there is no peace. The war is actually begun! The next gale that sweeps from the north will bring to our ears the clash of resounding arms! Our brethren are already in the field! Why stand we here idle? What is it that gentlemen wish? What would they have? Is life so dear, or peace so sweet, as to be purchased at the price of chains and slavery? Forbid it, Almighty God! I know not what course others may take; but as for me, give me liberty, or give me death![266]

Patrick Henry deserves a place in history, if for no other reason than for this speech.

CONCLUSION

The founders taught us courage, courage born of faith in God. It is a lesson to be heeded always.

Long after the United States became independent, we experienced our next major war, also with Great Britain—the War of 1812. During that time, our national anthem was born. On the night of Sept. 14, 1814 and dawn of Sept. 15, Francis Scott Key was an American held as a captive in a British ship during the War of 1812 in the Baltimore area. He was concerned during the battle to see if the American flag, the star-spangled banner, was still waving over the fort. . . . It was. He wrote the national anthem, and the 4th verse talked about our need to trust in the Lord:

> . . . Blest with victory and peace, may the heav'n-rescued land
> Praise the Power that hath made and preserved us a nation!
> Then conquer we must, when our cause, it is just,
> And this be our motto: "In God is our trust."

CHAPTER TEN

Justice
and the Courts

*The Constitution is a mere thing of wax
in the hands of the judiciary, which they may twist
and shape into any form they please.*[267]

Thomas Jefferson

Thomas Jefferson warned what can happen with runaway courts that legislate from the bench, instead of simply adjudicating: "The germ of dissolution of our federal government is in . . . the federal judiciary."[268] His concern was deepened by the fact that federal judges have lifetime tenure. He wrote, "You seem...to consider the judges as the ultimate arbiters of all constitutional questions; a very dangerous doctrine indeed, and one which would place us under the despotism of an oligarchy. Our judges are as honest as other men, and not more so...and their power [is] the more dangerous, as they are in office for life and not responsible, as the other functionaries are, to the elective control."[269]

Jefferson's concerns have proved correct. Name the issue today—abortion, pornography, loss of religious liberty, same-sex marriage, —and we find that it's generally the courts, many times the Supreme Court, that have legalized something contrary to God's will, and often contrary to the will of the people.

Writing in *Federalist* 49, James Madison said, "The members of the executive and judiciary departments are few in number, and can be personally known to a small part only of the people."[270] And he added, "The members of the legislative department, on the other hand, are numerous. They are distributed and dwell among the people at large."[271]

In *Federalist* 78, Alexander Hamilton said (in a footnote, no less), "The celebrated Montesquieu, speaking of them [the branches of government], says: "Of the three powers above mentioned, the judiciary is next to nothing."[272] In the same essay, Hamilton said, "It is not otherwise to be supposed, that the Constitution could intend to enable the representatives of the people to substitute their *will* to that of their constituents . . . . It is far more rational to suppose, that the courts were designed to be an intermediate body between the people and the legislature, in order, among other things, to keep the latter within the limits assigned to their authority. The interpretation of the laws is the proper and peculiar province of the courts."[273] In other words, the founders viewed the courts as interpreting laws, not writing them. They envisioned the justices adjudicating from the bench, not legislating from it. The founders inherited and continued a legal system that was based on the Scriptures. Let's consider in depth what the Bible says about the courts.

THE BIBLE AND THE COURTS

The Bible makes it clear that we should not pervert justice and there is a special concern for the poor. In Exodus 23:2-6, Moses declares:

> You shall not follow a crowd to do evil; nor shall you testify in a dispute so as to turn aside after many to pervert justice. You shall not show partiality to a poor man in his dispute. If you meet your enemy's ox or his donkey going astray, you shall surely bring it back to him again. If you see the donkey of one who hates you lying under its burden, and you would refrain from helping it, you shall surely help him with it. You shall not pervert the judgment of your poor in his dispute.

Modern America should heed these words. Often we see a scenario whereby a wealthy defendant can find the "best justice money can buy." If an ordinary citizen were similarly brought to trial for the same crime, he would usually not get off so easily. This is a great injustice. Justice is supposed to be blind—blind to how much money the defendant has, the color of his skin, level of his education, and so on.

WE ARE NOT TO TRAMPLE GOD'S COURTS

Isaiah the prophet makes it very clear that we are not to trample God's courts. In a sense, the judge is a substitute for God. Since he or she can even apply or commute the death sentence, a judge is actually sitting in God's place. Therefore, he must make sure he does not rule unjustly. Isaiah wrote about rulers who are rebels; judges who do not obey the law they have been set up to uphold. The bloodshed of the innocent makes a mockery of prayer he says, and the widow and the fatherless (people who are defenseless) are always God's concern. They should be ours too. The context shows that even their religiosity is rejected by God when they reject justice—including justice in the courts:

> Cease to do evil,
> Learn to do good;
> Seek justice,
> Rebuke the oppressor;
> Defend the fatherless,
> Plead for the widow. (Isaiah 1:16-17)

Let me use an obvious but extreme example. Suppose you have a man from the Mafia, responsible for all sorts of crimes, from murder to rape to prostitution to extortion to bribery of jury members to drug distribution, and so on. Now suppose the very same man goes to church and says prayers and donates money to the church. Is God pleased with that? Absolutely not.

When judges pervert justice for the sake of bribes, they are displeasing the Lord. When judges neglect the widow and the orphan and the underdog, they are displeasing the Lord. I think certainly a case can be made that the unborn child is among the most defenseless of us. In any event, God decries those who shed innocent blood. Abortion clearly is the shedding of innocent blood.

God continues through Isaiah to decry ancient Israel's lack of justice in the courts, a symptom of corruption at every level of society:

> How the faithful city has become a harlot!
> It was full of justice;
> Righteousness lodged in it,
> But now murderers.
> Your silver has become dross,
> Your wine mixed with water.
> Your princes are rebellious,
> And companions of thieves;
> Everyone loves bribes,

And follows after rewards.
They do not defend the fatherless,
Nor does the cause of the widow come before them.
(Isaiah 1:21-23)

God is looking for righteous judges who will uphold the law and help the weak and defenseless. I believe that even some liberal judges instinctively have learned that it is important to watch out for "the little guy," to help the underdog. This is a by-product of the Judeo-Christian ethic, a residue of which is still left in the culture, although it is fading fast. We should remember what G. K. Chesterton said. When a post-Christian culture takes one Christian virtue, say "mercy," and divorces it from other Christian virtues, say "justice," we can end up perverting both.

Take for example the ACLU. They claim that they are there to help the underdog, but they end up perverting true justice in virtually every case they take. Author George Grant points out:

> The ACLU's official position is that they are the watchdog for the underdog. They want to protect for instance, they say, the freedom of religion. But in fact, more often, they are more interested in freedom from religion, protecting the rights of atheists for instance, against believers. Their idea is that religion may very well be a dangerous thing, and must be contained and controlled. Freedom of religion is what the American founders were interested in. Freedom from religion is what the ACLU is interested in.[274]

Meanwhile, God is interested in justice in the courts, not the perversion thereof.

LET JUSTICE ROLL ON

The Bible says repeatedly that justice must not be denied the poor. This happens far too often in our society, and God loathes it. For example, Moses says: "You shall not pervert justice due the stranger or the fatherless, nor take a widow's garment as a pledge" (Deuteronomy 24:17).

The book of Amos is very clear on the same subject. The Lord declares through Amos:

> Hate evil, love good;
> Maintain justice in the courts.
> Perhaps the Lord God Almighty will be with you....
> But let justice roll on like a river,
> Righteousness like a never-failing stream. (Amos 5:15, 24 NIV)

In those days, judges would sit at the gates of the city. Those with complaints would come to sit before them. God was concerned that justice would be applied.

I find it interesting that one of the groups that sued Chief Justice Roy Moore, a righteous judge, to remove his Ten Commandments monument was the Southern Poverty Law Center. Their office in Montgomery was close to his former office. Ironically, they have a quote in stone on their building from Dr. Martin Luther King, Jr., "Let justice roll down." But they apparently don't realize Dr. King was simply quoting the Scriptures. Because of the misinterpretation of the First Amendment by the courts, the law has become terribly twisted in our time, and a righteous judge like Roy Moore can no longer sit on the bench.

EMINENT DOMAIN

In 2005, the U.S. Supreme Court made a ruling that shocked millions of Americans—conservatives and liberals alike. Eminent domain has always been in our system, for building hospitals and schools and the like. However, eminent domain has not been used to kick families out of their homes— perhaps homes owned by their families for generations—so that developers with high-powered lawyers can put up tax-revenue-generating commercial property.

The key Supreme Court eminent domain case is the *Kelo v.*

City of New London decision of 2005. It stemmed from a dispute over property rights in New London, Connecticut. Noted Christian attorney Jay Sekulow points out that this decision could have chilling effects on churches:

> Well, the city wanted more tax revenue. This was a case where the city engaged in eminent domain, not because the area was blighted, but because it was a tax revenue base increase. And the Supreme Court gave that a green light. Justice O'Connor wrote an interesting sentence. She said, "Under the Court's ruling a church could be taken for a shopping center, your private home for an apartment complex." And I think the real risk is not residential, although there are people's houses that have been taken subject to this new ruling, but the real threat is going to be against non-profits, specifically churches. . . . Well, the church issue is used because churches are exempt from property taxation in almost every state. The reason they're exempt is it was thought that churches gave more to the community than simply getting a tax benefit would have been. In other words, [it is as] if you would have gotten five thousand dollars' worth of tax benefits from the local church. Well, they give more to the community than that, so we'll give them an exemption from taxation. Well, now you look at that property that they're sitting on where the church is, and it's worth a lot of money; and you're already seeing this encroachment now where there's an increase of tax cases against religious organizations and churches to get tax revenue up. Eminent domain can make that quite a threat.[275]

We could be in for some difficult days ahead. We should strive to get judges who seek to apply justice in the courts, not injustice. This applies particularly to the poor. As I asked earlier, where are the evangelical judges in our time?

KEEPING THE GOSPEL LEGAL

We cannot build the kingdom of God on earth through political means. The best we can hope to do is to preserve religious liberty so that the Gospel may be preached. For example, we can fight to make sure Christianity never becomes illegal.

That may seem far fetched, but the forces of secular fundamentalism are uneasy with freedom for Christians. They do not mind if we sing our Christian hymns and songs in our church buildings. What they object to, for example, is Christians who have the gumption to declare that God does not approve of homosexuality. There are those in our culture who would punish any who do so—if they had the power. Look at what has happened in Canada or England to those who dare speak out about homosexuality as a sin. They have been accused of hate crimes.

For example, a Catholic city council member in British Columbia was a victim of vandalism by homosexual activists. Yet because he dared to say that homosexuality was "not normal or natural," he was forced to apologize and pay a $1,000 fine to a homosexual activist couple. Events like this in Canada and Europe could be a preview of coming attractions for this country.[276]

The late D. James Kennedy joined forces with the late Bill Bright of Campus Crusade for Christ, the late Larry Burkett, Dr. James Dobson, and several others to found the Alliance Defense Fund, a Christian-liberties legal group. They have been very effective in their key goal—to keep it legal to proclaim the Gospel in America. But they have a fight on their hands as the courts continue to erode our freedoms.

What have been the results of the courts making laws versus simply interpreting them? We have seen them chip away the remaining vestiges of our nation's rich Judeo-Christian heritage. Consider a recent example.

FREEDOM *FROM* RELIGION

The secular fundamentalists are at it again. This time they

are suing to remove a 57-year old cross in San Diego that serves as a veterans' memorial.

A three-judge panel in the U.S. 9th Circuit Court of Appeals, located in the San Francisco area, ruled in January 2011 that the tall, concrete cross at Mt. Soledad is unconstitutional. The ACLU filed suit on behalf of a Jewish group of veterans to remove the symbol.

The founders gave us freedom of religion. But the secular fundamentalists are moving us toward freedom from religion.

There's a huge difference. Freedom *of* religion gives freedom to all, regardless of what they believe. Freedom *from* religion discriminates against the believer. Plus, in any country where atheism is officially established, anyone who disagrees with the ruling party (or usually dictator) is on the outs—even if he too is an atheist.

Stalin, the arch-atheist, had Leon Trotsky, another arch-atheist, Communist, and co-architect of the Soviet Union, hunted down all across the globe. Finally, in Mexico, one of Stalin's followers managed to slam an ice axe into Trotsky's brain.

Ideas have consequences.

Why can't we learn from the failed Soviet Union? Its official atheism unleashed a huge 70-year nightmare of bloodshed on the people of Russian and adjoining nations.

America is predicated on one thing: Our rights come from God. That's what the Declaration of Independence says. The Constitution is predicated on the Declaration. Our 1776 birth certificate explains why we exist. The Constitution then explains how our government is to work.

When rights come from God, they are non-negotiable.

But secular fundamentalists do everything they can to strip away our Judeo-Christian heritage. They've been so successful that many of our schools have become something Bill Clinton spoke against—"religion-free zones."

A valedictorian can thank any power or person or force he or she wants to—unless it's the G-word or worse, the J-word. One valedictorian actually had her microphone cut off in the middle of her speech because the authorities feared she was going to thank Jesus Christ for his help. Score another one for the secular fundamentalists.

If the secular fundamentalists were successful in their goal to purge any reference to God or our Judeo-Christian heritage from public life, eventually they would have to scrub the Constitution itself. That document mentions God. It even acknowledges the Deity of Jesus Christ. How so you ask. It is signed "in the year of our Lord," as in our Lord Jesus Christ. But that's just a tradition, you might say. It doesn't mean anything. If the fact that our Western calendar is based on the birth of Jesus means nothing, then why did the atheistic leaders of the French Revolution decide to toss out the calendar and make the year 1791 into Year 1 of the Republic? In an effort to remove all Judeo-Christian influences, the Revolutionaries even abandoned the 7-day week with its built-in sabbaths—Saturday for Jews and the Lord's Day for the Christians—opting for a 10-day week. (Thankfully, Napoleon undid all these things.)

The secular fundamentalists had their way in the French Revolution, and the streets of Paris ran red with blood. The secular fundamentalists had their way in the Soviet Union and in China and in Cambodia, etc., and *The Black Book of Communism*[277] documents the Communist atrocities that killed 100 million people in the 20th Century.

The scrubbing of all Judeo-Christian symbols from the public square is just another attack on our civilization from the secular fundamentalists. What's next? The crosses at Arlington?

OUR ROBED MASTERS

If anybody takes a half hour or so to actually read the Constitution, he will see that the founders said much more about the legislative and executive branches than they did the judicial branch. The founders never envisioned the day—nor would they have countenanced it—where we are essentially ruled by our robed masters.

Every year, around early June, we have to wait for the Supreme Court—like robed gods and goddess descending from Mount Olympus—to tell us what our rights are. Many of these decisions are hotly contested. Some of them boil down to one key swing vote. As of this writing, Anthony Kennedy is that swing vote. He has certainly disappointed conservatives with some key decisions in favor of abortion or homosexuality.

Consider what the courts have ushered in:

- pornography on demand, (*Roth v. United States*, 1957) and *Miller v. California*, 1973).
- no school prayer allowed (*Engel v. Vitale*, 1962, and *Murray v. Curlette*, 1963).
- no official Bible reading of a devotional nature in schools (*Abington v. Schempp*, 1963).
- abortion on demand, through *Roe v. Wade*, 1973, which dissenting Justice Byron White called an act of "raw judicial power." *Roe* was based on a series of lies, and today the Roe in this case, Jane McCorvey, is pro-life and has even tried to get the case overturned. Meanwhile, as of this writing, more than 50 million Americans have been killed through abortion because of this one decision by seven men.
- no Ten Commandments to be posted in the schools (*Stone v. Graham*, 1980). They actually said in that decision:

If the posted copies of the Ten Commandments are to have any effect at all, it will be to induce the schoolchildren to read, meditate upon, perhaps to venerate and obey, the Commandments. However desirable this might be as a matter of private devotion, it is not a permissible state objective under the Establishment Clause.[278]

- no equal time for creation science in the classroom (*Edwards v. Aguilard*, 1987).
- states are not free (as in the case of Colorado) to prohibit the grant of special legal rights to homosexuals (*Romer v. Evans*, 1996).
- states are not free (as in the case of Texas)

to outlaw sodomy (*Lawrence v. Texas*, 2003). This decision was used by the Massachusetts Supreme Court when it took the next logical step and granted the right to same-sex marriage.

- colleges (or law schools, as in this case) are free to oust a Christian group from campus, if it will not allow for homosexuals to be among their leaders (*Martinez v. Hastings*, 2010).

And on it goes.

We were not intended to be ruled by the High Court. The founders clearly denounced monarchy—rule by the king, as well as oligarchy—rule by the few.

CONCLUSION

In 1861, when President Lincoln was sworn in, in one of the great ironies of history, it was Roger Taney who administered the oath. Taney, the Chief Justice of the Supreme Court, was the very man who had written the aptly named *Dred Scott* decision, which effectively held that "once a slave always a slave," and a former slave who had been recaptured had no rights under the Constitution.

When Lincoln delivered his First Inaugural Address, he eschewed the idea that we the people should be ruled by "we the judges." I'm sure he had the *Dred Scott* decision in mind, when he said the following: "If the policy of the Government upon vital questions affecting the whole people is to be irrevocably fixed by decisions of the Supreme Court, the instant they are made in ordinary litigation between parties in personal actions the people will have ceased to be their own rulers, having to that extent practically resigned their Government into the hands of that eminent tribunal."[279] In other words, he didn't buy the premise upon which judicial activism was built. Nor should we.

CHAPTER ELEVEN

Economic Prosperity

*[T]he most productive system of finance
will always be the least burdensome.*[280]

Alexander Hamilton

Alexander Hamilton was our first Secretary of the Treasury, and he said in *Federalist 35* that our economy will work best when we have less needless regulation. Today we are monstrously in debt and borrowing more and more off the backs of our children and grandchildren.

Think of the sacrifice of the founding fathers for our behalf. As John Adams once said, "Posterity! You will never know how much it cost the present generation to preserve your freedom! I hope you will make good use of it! If you do not, I shall repent it in Heaven that I ever took half the pains to preserve it!"[281]

Samuel Adams said, "If ye love wealth better than liberty, the tranquillity of servitude than the animating contest of freedom, go from us in peace. We ask not your counsels or arms. Crouch down and lick the hands which feed you. May your chains sit lightly upon you, and may posterity forget that ye were our countrymen."[282]

In his Farewell Address, George Washington warned the new nation to be careful about national debt:

> As a very important source of strength and security, cherish public credit. One method of preserving it is to use it as sparingly as possible, avoiding occasions of expense by cultivating peace, but remembering also that timely disbursements to prepare for danger frequently prevent much greater disbursements to repel it, avoiding likewise the accumulation of debt, not only by shunning occasions of expense, but by vigorous exertion in time of peace to discharge the debts which unavoidable wars may have occasioned, not ungenerously throwing upon posterity the burden which we ourselves ought to bear.[283]

Thomas Jefferson also gave some strong warnings about our economy. In his First Inaugural Address, our third president said, "a wise and frugal Government, which shall restrain men from injuring one another, shall leave them otherwise free to regulate their own pursuits of industry and improvement, and shall not take from the mouth of labor the bread it has earned.

This is the sum of good government."[284]

Notice in particular what Jefferson had to say about governmental debt:

"I am for a government rigorously frugal and simple, applying all the possible savings of the public revenue to the discharge of the national debt; and not for a multiplication of officers and salaries merely to make partisans, and for increasing, by every device, the public debt, on the principle of its being public blessing."[285] One can only imagine what Jefferson would think of our bloated government today.

James Madison said, "I go on the principle that a public debt is a public curse, and in a Republican Government a greater curse than in any other."[286]

Beyond the founding era, in the early 1800s, someone astutely predicted: "America will last until the populace discovers that it can vote for itself largesse out of the public treasury."[287] What this saying means is that America will last until people realize they can vote gifts or handouts from the public treasury for themselves. Sadly, modern Americans have discovered this all too well.

THE BOSTON TEA PARTY

On the night of Dec. 16, 1773, in Boston harbor, the American Sons of Liberty, led by Christian patriot Sam Adams, protested the unfair tax policies of the British against the colonists. They threw 342 chests of tea off a British ship into the Boston Harbor in the famous Boston Tea Party.

We keep hearing today about the Tea Party movement. Of course, it is a modern rebirth of the Boston Tea Party. It's interesting to note that the key leader of the first tea party movement said that Jesus Christ is the source of our rights. "The Rights of the Colonists" was an historic statement by Sam Adams written in 1772. It is viewed as one of the key forerunners articulating why America should sever its ties to Great Britain. In this document, Samuel Adams included a section entitled, "The Rights of the Colonist as Christians," in which he declared: "The right to freedom being the gift of God

Almighty, the rights of the Colonists as Christians may best be understood by reading and carefully studying the institutions of The Great Law Giver and the Head of the Christian Church, which are to be found clearly written and promulgated in the New Testament."[288]

It's interesting to note, too, that Dr. Martin Luther King, Jr. mentioned that rebellious act in one of his speeches. He said, "Our nation in a sense came into being through a massive act of civil disobedience for the Boston Tea Party was nothing but a massive act of civil disobedience."[289]

THE TEA PARTY MOVEMENT

My congressman, Allen West, is a great guy. He's a war hero who has spoken at Tea Party events. He told me recently that the federal government is becoming like a "crack addict." Rep. West said, "They're just addicted to the money that is not theirs. When you go up to Washington, D.C., you see construction cranes all over the place, you see growth in Washington, D.C., but then when you come down here to our congressional district, and you go up and down US Highway 1, you see empty storefronts. So, there is a transfer of wealth from the people that are on the ground here, who can create jobs and opportunities and things of that nature, and it goes up north, to Washington, D.C."[290]

The fact that 47% of Americans do not pay federal income taxes is a "dangerous thing," West said, and a consequence of our progressive tax system which "has created a class warfare in the United States of America. It is pitting a certain group of people against another group of people."[291]

I said to him, "Well, somebody once said, if you rob Peter to pay Paul, you can always count on Paul's support politically."

West responded, "And that's exactly what's happened, what's happening. We will see a reshaping of national level elections if we continue on with this system of class warfare that has been implemented through out taxation system."[292]

The Bible, of course, teaches that we should pay our taxes. Jesus said, Render unto Caesar the things that are Caesar's and unto God the things that are God's. The Bible also teaches in 1 Samuel 8, that excessive, outrageous taxation can occur when a people turn their back on God.

Democratic Congressman Mike McIntyre of North Carolina points out that part of the reason Americans are overtaxed today is because too many in our society view government as the solution to everything.

> I think the bottom line is, is that for those of us in Congress, we have to be responsible as stewards of the taxpayers' money. And that means we've got to be good trustees and there's got to be transparency, there's got to be accountability for how taxpayer dollars are spent, and you've got to make sure that we're getting the wisest use out of tax dollars, the wisest investment, and that government is not the solution to everything.[293]

AN ILLUSTRATION FROM DR. KENNEDY

The late Dr. D. James Kennedy once gave a powerful anecdote concerning producers versus takers, government regulations, and basic economics:

> Let me give an illustration about a fictitious village which existed on top of a cliff. Three or four hundred feet down from this cliff was a river. Every day each family had to spend about two hours of their time going down with buckets, filling them with water for drinking, cooking, washing, and for the animals, and then carrying the water up the steep incline. Finally, one man had an idea. He noticed that the river, when its flow was about five miles back up in the jungle, was higher than the cliff. He thought that if he could somehow get a pipe from that river down to the village, he could bring water to the village, and people would not have this hard chore. So every evening, after working on the farm, he would cut large pieces of bamboo and fit them together. He worked on this

for years and years. Finally he had five miles of this bamboo pipe which he put into the river above the village. While everybody excitedly watched, water flowed into a reservoir which he had made in the center of the village.

He charged the people something for all of his labor. He charged them the equivalent of fifteen minutes of their time per day, and they rejoiced in this. No more was there the backbreaking two hours of labor every day to get the water. Everybody had enough water, and the whole village flourished because of this.

Then someone said, "Why should he have more than the rest of us? He does not do anything. What we ought to do is put a tax on his pipeline. And then we can have part of his wealth, and we will be better off." A brilliant idea, no doubt. So they put a tax on the pipeline, and the next year they increased the tax.

He had been involved in repairing the pipeline from time to time as it broke down, but as they increased the tax still more, it got to the place where it was not even profitable for him to own the pipeline anymore. So the next time it broke down, he did not bother with it. And the whole thing collapsed, and the reservoir became empty. The village began to whither from the lack of water. The crops diminished. The people went back to spending two hours a day going down and drawing water. You see, he had, in fact, lifted the living conditions of the whole of the village, and he had become wealthy in the process. There is a biblical principle behind that. Jesus said it: "he who is greatest among you shall be your servant" (Matthew 23:11). Henry Ford made millions and millions of dollars, and yet he enriched the lives of everyone.[294]

Dr. Kennedy also noted that a major part of the problem with the economy today is with "we the people." More than half the population has gotten addicted to government freebies—

not thinking about the fact that those have to be paid for by the sweat and blood of the productive. Dr. Kennedy and I wrote:

> The problem is with us—with our own hearts, our own greed, our own desires for something for nothing—for more and more and more from the government trough. That is the problem. That is why the politicians act that way. If your eyes were opened and you saw the colossal wastefulness, if you saw the mounting federal debt which could destroy us as a nation, if you saw the inefficiency and ineffectiveness of these government programs, then when a politician tells you he is going to tax more and spend more, he would not get your vote. But if he told you he was going to cut taxes and spending, he would have your vote and he would stay in office.
>
> Someone studied witnesses that come to congressional committees to make their proposals. For every one who comes and says, "We need to cut taxes and cut spending," there are 134 who come and tell them, "Spend more. Spend more. We want more, more, more from the federal government." Remember. The federal government does not have anything to begin with. It all comes out of our pockets.
>
> I believe that Jesus would encourage private, church-based, community-based giving and help. I also believe He would not favor governmental programs. The government programs are bloated and inefficient. Frankly, they have a vested interest in the poverty continuing because if they do not, then the bureaucrats are out of a job.
>
> Let the government get out of the charity business, and let the family, church, and community be free to take care of the less fortunate. I believe we should vote in accordance with true justice and not the mistaken notion of "social justice." It is time to stop falling for the politician who essentially tries to buy our vote.
>
> It is one thing to say Jesus would have us do

more than our fair share for the poor. It is another thing to say that He would have us force such "generosity" on the population at large through the fist of government.[295]

RUNAWAY GOVERNMENT SPENDING

Just before the 2010 midterm elections, comedians Jon Stewart and Steven Colbert organized their DC rally of about 60,000 people, a rally held for "restoring sanity." Obviously, this was playing off of Glenn Beck's "Restoring Honor" rally.

A sub-rally within that gathering was a march for government workers. It was organized by Steve Ressler who heads "GovLoop," a website for government workers. The name of the march Ressler organized is crude: it was the "Government Doesn't S**k" march." Ressler said, "We hear it day in and day out: the government s**ks, federal employees are lazy and their positions are redundant." He added, "It's time to turn the tables and remind the world that government employees just happen to be people—people that don't s**k."

I'm sure there are a lot of nice people who work for Uncle Sam; the problem is that there are too many of them. The government has gotten too big, and the tab to pay for government services keeps adding up and will have to be paid by our children and grandchildren.

Government is growing more and more under the current administration and Congressional leaders. The only way we the people can fight back at their socialistic push is at the ballot box.

The dirty little secret about socialism is that it fails every time.

Ronald Reagan used to collect jokes that Russians would tell each other during the heyday of the Soviet Union. They told these funny stories to try and ameliorate the misery of living under Communism. Here's one of the jokes. The context is how difficult it was to acquire a car under the Communists. You had to go through all sorts of bureaucratic hoops, and at most, only one out of seven Soviet citizens ever got one. You also had to pay *years* in advance. So one day, a man fulfilled all the obligations, including paying all the money up front. The bureaucrat told him that he had successfully completed his paperwork, and he would get his car in ten years. The man asked, "In the morning or the afternoon?" The bureaucrat was taken aback and replied, "It's ten years from now. What do you care whether it's the morning or the afternoon?" The man said, "Well, I've got the plumber coming in the morning."

Socialism doesn't work now, and it has never worked. In his book, *Heaven on Earth: The Rise and Fall of Socialism,* Joshua Muravchik says, "From New Harmony to Moscow, from Dar es Salaam to London, the story of socialism was the story of a dream unrealized, a word that would not be made flesh."[296]

I remember hearing Reagan say in 1984—how much worse it is now in 2010—that the Congress was spending money like drunken sailors. Then he added that he must apologize to the Navy men because at least the sailors were spending their *own* money.

Flash forward to today. Because of the reckless spending of Congress, the U.S. government now owes nearly $15 trillion (as of this writing). The debt keeps increasing, at a rate of about $2 million a minute. How can that ever get paid back? The federal government is bankrupting future generations. And we're letting them get away with it.

I heard a speaker recently, who said that debt that gets into the *trillions* of dollars is totally out of control. He gave the following illustration to help grasp how much a trillion is, say, in comparison with a million.

> If I owed you $100 and said I'd pay you in a million seconds, when would I pay you? In 12 days.
> If I owed you $100 and said I'd pay you in a billion seconds, when would I pay you? In 32 years.
> If I owed you $100 and said I'd pay you in a trillion seconds, when would I pay you? In 32,000 years.

Reagan once quipped that the closest thing to eternal life on this earth is a government program. So the chances of stopping all the reckless Congressional spending are an uphill battle. But it's a battle worth fighting.

THE NATIONAL DEBT—A MORAL ISSUE?

America's national debt is truly a moral issue. The Bible says the borrower is a slave to the lender. It also says that, as much as is possible, we should try to avoid debt—except the debt to love one another. Furthermore, it notes that a good man leaves an inheritance for his children.

But today in America, we're leaving a pile of debt for our children. How is that good?

This reminds me of the joke going around about a year ago: "Have you heard about the new Obama McDonald's special? You order everything you want, and then the guy behind you pays the bill."

What kind of a country runs up a big bill, spends the money now, and then leaves it up to our children and grandchildren to have to pay it all back? There is nothing ethical about this.

Rep. Michele Bachmann (R-MN) said in an interview with Coral Ridge Ministries (now Truth in Action Ministries) that "The national debt is a moral issue, because it is affecting every man, woman, and child in this country. We're at a very dangerous point now with the escalation of debt in our country. We've never before seen this level of debt."[297]

Rep. Mike Pence (R-IN) of Indiana said, "We have to make sacrifices that affect us today and put us on a long term pathway of fiscal solvency, rather than enjoying the blessings of prosperity today, but bequeathing to our children and grandchildren the obligations to figure out how to pay for it."[298]

The fact is, we all have to live within our means. Why should the government be any different? Liberals will say we need to do more to help the poor. I agree. But on a *voluntary* basis. And I do my part. But the government doesn't truly help the poor—it only makes more of them—for example, by subsidizing illegitimacy.

Could it be that such government programs are essentially trying to buy votes? Hopefully, we will get this runaway government spending under control before we bankrupt the nation—and leave our children stuck with the bill.

To me, runaway government spending, in general, is like a father going into his three-year old's room, breaking open her piggy bank, stealing all the money, and leaving a note. Not an IOU. But a UO-me.

The debt is now $14.7 trillion. With some 311 million Americans, this means each of us—man, woman, child, newborn baby—owes more than $47,000 now. Ouch. (And when all the unfunded liabilities, such as all the entitlement promises made by the U.S. government, are added up, then the debt exceeds $60 trillion. Totally unsustainable.) As Scriptures states, a wise man leaves an inheritance for his children—not massive debt (Proverbs 13:22).

As a prominent politician said a few years ago:

> The fact that we are here today to debate raising America's debt limit is a sign of leadership failure. It is a sign that the U.S. Government can not pay its own bills. It is a sign that we now depend on ongoing financial assistance from foreign countries to finance our Government's reckless fiscal policies. Increasing America's debt weakens us domestically and internationally. Leadership means that, "the buck stops here." Instead, Washington is shifting the burden of bad choices today onto the backs of our children and grandchildren. America has a debt problem and a failure of leadership. Americans deserve better.[299]

Which prominent politician said that? Senator Barack Obama in March 2006.

The way our government spends *future* money reminds me of a classic scene from a W. C. Fields movie in which he walks into a saloon and asks, "Was I, by chance, in here last night and did I have a $20 bill?"

"Oh yes," replies the bartender, "You spent the whole thing."

"Oh, what a load off my mind," says W. C. Fields. "I thought I had lost it!"

THE LAND OF THE ADDICTED AND THE HOME OF THE CRAVEN

Our nation is at serious risk because the government continues to overspend. We are heading for a showdown. Our government officials don't know when to stop spending—*other people's money*. But finally, in the summer of 2011, Congress did something partially right. They voted to not increase the debt ceiling—unless there was also a commitment to decrease spending. I heard the pundits said it was just a symbolic vote. Well, if that's true, they chose the right symbol to send.

So many in Congress are addicted to spending. I think they should start mandatory meetings of Overspenders Anonymous on Capitol Hill for our Representatives and Senators—*and* the President and his cabinet.

"My name is Congressman Bob, [Crowd: "Hello, Bob"] and I'm addicted to spending other people's money. . . ." Seriously, this is out of hand and every American should be alarmed.

It seems that all real efforts to put off this reckless course are mischaracterized. For example, Congressman Paul Ryan is trying to save Medicare, but he's being falsely accused of trying to ruin it. His plan increases Medicare spending over time, just not at the projected rate of growth.

It's time for many politicians (not Paul Ryan) to join Overspenders Anonymous. It's time for us back home to stop clamoring, "Give me. Give me."

It has been said that government is not a producer; it's a taker. The government has no money of its own. Every tax dollar came from someone, and most of it came by force. If you don't think it's by force, then look at the example the IRS makes of those who choose not to pay. It's a telling irony that Eliot Ness couldn't nab Al Capone, but the IRS sure did.

The late author and financial expert Larry Burkett once noted, "In our society today you can borrow to buy things that you can't afford to own. And credit doesn't eliminate the decision that you can't afford to own—it only delays it and makes it worse. . . ." Why is it hard for anybody to see that the government can't keep spending money like there's no tomorrow?

It's like dieting. If you insist on eating an apple fritter, then be prepared to make some other concession in your diet or exercise schedule to compensate for it. Or be prepared for such splurging to show up on your waistline.

We just can't keep spending and not expect to pay the piper.

CONCLUSION

Proverbs 13:22 says "A good man leaves an inheritance for his children's children." In America we're now doing the opposite—contrary to what both the Bible and the founders had to say.

On our TV segment on the immorality of the national debt, author Bill Federer made the observation, "Our founders were willing to sacrifice their prosperity for their posterity. They pledged their lives and their fortunes and their sacred honor for their posterity. Today, we're sacrificing our posterity for prosperity and saddling our kids with an unpayable debt, so we can maintain our standard of living."[300]

CHAPTER TWELVE

A Nation in Need
of Prayer

*I have lived, Sir, a long time,
and the longer I live, the more convincing proofs
I see of this truth—that God governs the affairs
of men. And if a sparrow cannot fall to the ground
without His notice, is it probable that an
empire can rise without His aid?*[301]

Benjamin Franklin

Amerika was born out of a spiritual renewal, known as the Great Awakening. Author Robert Flood reports that between 1740 and 1742, out of a total population of 300,000 souls in New England, 25,000 to 50,000 people joined the churches. "The movement changed the entire moral tone of New England for the better and justly earned the name of a 'Great Awakening.'"[302]

One of the best-known preachers of the Great Awakening was Jonathan Edwards, who preached in Northampton, Massachusetts, where, under his ministry, the whole movement was born. Later, George Whitefield from England helped spread the movement up and down the Atlantic Coast. Ben Franklin described the effects of Whitefield's preaching in his *Autobiography*:

> It was wonderful to see the change soon made in the manners of our inhabitants. From being thoughtless or indifferent about religion, it seemed as if all the world were growing religious, so that one could not walk through the town in an evening without hearing psalms sung in different families of every street.[303]

Historian Paul Johnson writes that the Great Awakening was first and foremost a spiritual movement with "undoubted political undertones."[304] Johnson attributes enormous significance to the Great Awakening. He calls it "the proto-revolutionary event, the formative movement in American history, preceding the political drive for independence, and making it possible."[305]

John Adams, as Johnson notes, credited the Great Awakening for what came later: "The Revolution was effected before the War commenced. The Revolution was in the mind and hearts of the people: and change in their religious sentiments of their duties and obligations."[306]

According to Johnson, "The Revolution could not have taken place without this religious background. The essential difference between the American Revolution and the French

Revolution is that the American Revolution, in its origins, was a religious event, whereas the French Revolution was an anti-religious event."[307]

DAYS OF FASTING AND PRAYER

During the war, Congress called for days of fasting and prayer to ask for God's help in the crisis. On the 15th of April, 1775, just days before Lexington, John Hancock, the president of the Massachusetts Provincial Congress, declared a "Day of Public Humiliation, Fasting and Prayer." This is what Mr. Hancock wrote in this proclamation:

> In circumstances dark as these, it becomes us, as Men and Christians, to reflect that, whilst every prudent Measure should be taken to ward the impending Judgements. . . . All confidence must be withheld from the Means we use; and reposed only on that GOD who rules in the Armies of Heaven, and without whose Blessing the best human Counsels are but Foolishness—and all created Power Vanity; It is the Happiness of his Church that, when the Powers of Earth and Hell combine against it . . . that the Throne of Grace is of the easiest access—and its Appeal thither is graciously invited by the Father of Mercies, who has assured it, that when his Children ask Bread he will not give them a Stone. . . .
>
> RESOLVED, That it be, and hereby is recommended to the good People of this Colony of all Denominations, that THURSDAY the Eleventh Day of May next be set apart as a Day of Public Humiliation, Fasting and Prayer . . . to confess the sins . . . to implore the Forgiveness of all our Transgression . . . and a blessing on the Husbandry, Manufactures, and other lawful Employments of this People; and especially that the union of the American Colonies in Defence of their Rights (for hitherto we desire to thank Almighty GOD) may be preserved and confirmed. . . . And that AMERICA may soon behold a gracious Interposition of

Heaven.
By Order of the Provincial Congress,
John Hancock, President.[308]

Here is another example of a Proclamation of a Day of Fasting and Prayer. This comes from the colony of Connecticut. Note the date of this was April 19, 1775. We're not sure if the authors of the Proclamation had already heard the news from Lexington and Concord, but it's certainly possible that they had heard about Lexington, since that battle happened early in the morning. Connecticut Governor Jonathan Trumbull prayed that:

> God would graciously pour out His Holy Spirit on us to bring us to a thorough Repentance and effectual Reformation that our iniquities may not be our ruin; that He would restore, preserve and secure the Liberties of this and all the other British American colonies, and make the Land a mountain of Holiness, and Habitation of Righteousness forever.[309]

Such proclamations acknowledged that prayer was essential to the American cause.

CONSTITUTIONAL CONVENTION

During the writing of the Constitution, things went slowly and the delegates became mired down in the difficult task. Finally, after weeks of little progress, Ben Franklin gave a pivotal speech on June 28, 1787. He began, by addressing George Washington, who presided over the proceedings:

> Mr. President:
> The small progress we have made after 4 or 5 weeks close attendance [prior to that was sparse attendance, not even enough for a quorum] & continual reasonings with each other—our different sentiments on almost every question, several of the last producing as many noes as ayes,

is methinks a melancholy proof of the imperfection
of the Human Understanding.

Franklin went on to remind his hearers that a decade
before they had prayers in that very room—Independence
Hall in Philadelphia:

> In the beginning of the Contest with G[reat]
> Britain, when we were sensible of danger, we had
> daily prayer in this room for Divine protection—
> Our prayers, Sir, were heard, & they were graciously
> answered. All of us who were engaged in the
> struggle must have observed frequent instances of a
> superintending Providence in our favor.

Now, all these years later, says Franklin, we can
thank God for the chance to create a new government
in peace:

> To that kind Providence we owe this happy
> opportunity of consulting in peace on the means of
> establishing our future national felicity. And have
> we now forgotten that powerful Friend? or do we
> imagine we no longer need His assistance?
>
> I have lived, Sir, a long time, and the longer
> I live, the more convincing proofs I see of this
> truth—that God Governs in the affairs of men. And
> if a sparrow cannot fall to the ground without His
> notice, is it probable that an empire can rise without
> His aid?
>
> We have been assured, Sir, in the Sacred
> Writings, that "except the Lord build the House, they
> labor in vain that build it." I firmly believe this; and I
> also believe that without his concurring aid we shall
> succeed in this political building no better than the
> Builders of Babel: We shall be divided by our partial
> local interests; our projects will be confounded, and
> we ourselves shall become a reproach and bye word
> down to future ages.[310]

Franklin continued by offering a specific motion that they have prayer at the convention. His request was adopted in modified form, and their previous impasse was broken. New Jersey delegate Jonathan Dayton provided an eyewitness report of the reaction to Dr. Franklin's impassioned request for prayer:

> The Doctor sat down; and never did I behold a countenance at once so dignified and delighted as was that of Washington at the close of the address; nor were the members of the convention generally less affected. The words of the venerable Franklin fell upon our ears with a weight and authority, even greater that we may suppose an oracle to have had in a Roman senate![311]

But, as John Eidsmoe, author of *Christianity and the Constitution,* explains:

> The motion for opening the sessions with prayer every morning was not acted on because the Convention lacked funds to pay a clergyman, and because the delegates were afraid that news of outside clergymen coming to assist in services would start rumors that dissension was breaking out in the Convention.[312]

However, Edmund Jennings Randolph of Virginia came up with a compromise measure, which fulfilled the essence of Franklin's request. Randolph proposed: "That a sermon be preached at the request of the convention on the 4th of July, the anniversary of Independence; & thenceforward prayers be used in ye Convention every morning."[313] Ben Franklin himself seconded this substitute motion. So while Franklin's initial request was not officially acted upon, it was not officially rejected.

The spirit of the request was carried out and the impasse was broken. Delegate Dayton of New Jersey reported that when the delegates met again on July 2, much of the acrimony was gone: "We assembled again; and . . . every unfriendly feeling had been expelled, and a spirit of conciliation had been cultivated."[314]

The entire assembly worshiped together at the Reformed Calvinistic Lutheran Church in Philadelphia on July 4th. While some difficulties still arose before the conclusion of the Convention's business in September, the delegates apparently never returned to the fruitless acrimony that had existed prior to June 28th.

AN EXAMPLE IN OUR TIME OF HOW PRAYER CAN CHANGE THINGS

A few years before he died, Dr. D. James Kennedy made an impassioned plea for Christians to pray for a Third Great Awakening—our nation's only real hope. He said, "I believe that if America is to ever be a Christian nation again, we need to return to our roots."

Prayer is powerful. Let's take a moment to look at a recent example of a vexing issue, abortion, where prayer is making a great impact.

A relatively new outreach, "40 Days for Life," has been organizing a 24-hour, seven-day a week commitment to pray for forty consecutive days in select cities. David Bereit, the National Director of 40 Days for Life, notes, "We've had now eight nationally coordinated campaigns. Each of those is made up of local campaigns. There have been 1,332 local campaigns that have taken place in 387 cities, and that's been in all 50 American states, as well as Canada, Australia, England, Ireland, northern Ireland, Spain, Denmark, the country of Georgia, Armenia and Belize."

Based in Fredericksburg, Virginia, this organization has seen incredible results since they began in 2004. They claim that, so far, at least 4,313 babies (that they know of) have been saved from abortion. That's 4,313 babies who are bringing joy to their mothers, whether by birth or by adoption.

40 Days for Life also claims that 53 clinic workers have

had a change of heart because of these vigils and have left the abortion field as a result. The most famous of them is Abby Johnson, former director of the Planned Parenthood clinic of Bryan, Texas. When she saw a sonogram of an abortion, she walked away from the business. She had no idea where to go or what to do, but she saw the pro-life people silently praying in front of the clinic she directed and sought them out. She has since written a book about her whole change of heart—*Unplanned.*

Thanks to their efforts, says 40 Days for Life, thirteen abortion centers have shut down. Again, this is all because of peaceful prayer vigils held around the clock for forty consecutive days in selected cities.

It may be just a coincidence that these abortion centers closed their doors during the time of the 40-day-long prayer meetings. On the other hand, someone once described a coincidence as "a miracle where God chooses to remain anonymous."

Bereit believes that the time is ripe for change in America's view of abortion. "So we're seeing the abortion industry on a rapid decline right now, and if ever there were a time for people of faith and conscience to take action to do something to speak up for those that cannot speak for themselves, I really believe that time is right now."

There indeed may be a shift in Americans' views in this area. For example, a recent Gallup poll conducted in May 2011 found that 51% of Americans believe abortion is "morally wrong," while 39% view it as "morally acceptable."

The numbers are even higher when it comes to opposition to publically funded abortion. Many Americans who identify themselves as pro-choice oppose their tax-dollars' paying for it. They think, "If you want to have an abortion, that's your business—but don't make me pay for it."

Across America, there are now more pro-life pregnancy centers, which provide free services for women with unplanned pregnancies than there are sites where abortions are performed. Bereit says, "In most communities in America there are now Christian pregnancy help centers, and there are 2,300 of these now; whereas, the abortion industry is down to 672." Sadly, however, there are still more abortions being done in those 672 clinics than the number of babies that are being saved in the 2,300 centers.

When you look in the yellow pages under abortion, it's often a mix between pregnancy centers—offering pro-life alternatives to abortion—and abortion clinics. How do you tell the difference between the two? My friend Janet (Folger) Porter says that's easy. Just look for the credit card logos. The abortion clinics have them; the pregnancy centers don't. One is a business; the other is charity funded by volunteer donations.

Abortion is primarily about money—and lots of it. But it has been, is now, and always will be blood money.

Thankfully, groups like 40 Days for Life may well be helping to change the landscape in America when it comes to abortion—one prayer at a time.

CONCLUSION

Let's close with the insights of founding father John Hancock, who presided over the very same Continental Congress that gave us the Declaration of Independence. Hancock later became governor of Massachusetts, and in 1791 he declared a statewide proclamation of public thanksgiving to Almighty God. He thanked God for all sorts of blessings that He had poured out, but above all he was thankful for sending His Son, and he longed for the earthly kingdom of Christ to be established. We thank God for many blessings, writes Hancock,

> . . . but the great and most important Blessing, the Gospel of Jesus Christ: And together with our cordial acknowledgments, I do earnestly recommend, that we may join the penitent confession of our Sins, and implore the further continuance of the Divine Protection, and Blessings of Heaven upon this People . . . that all may bow to the Scepter of our LORD JESUS CHRIST, and the whole Earth be filled with his Glory [emphasis his].[315]

Our founding fathers have so much to teach us. Above all, they teach that we should stop turning our backs on our Almighty God. We could easily put it this way: We should never expect God's blessings if we continue to defy His Word. George Washington said as much in his First Inaugural Address: "The propitious smiles of Heaven can never be expected on a nation that disregards the eternal rules of order and right which Heaven itself has ordained."[316]

I believe, as did the late Dr. D. James Kennedy, that America's only real hope lies in true revival. Here are his words spoken in front of the Lincoln Memorial in 2003:

> Too often we forget that America became a nation soon after a spiritual revival, the First Great Awakening. Then in the 1800s, America experienced a Second Great Awakening, which helped bring about a moral revolution—particularly in addressing the evil of slavery. But now we are in need of a Third Great Awakening. Will you join me in praying for that? Many people are under the misconception that government will solve all our problems. But I believe that true change is going to take place when people throughout the nation begin to trust in Christ and in the God that made this nation great. And that will bring about a genuine revival. A revival that eventually moves to the halls of government. Not from the government down, but from the people up. God once declared, "If my people, which are called by my name, shall humble themselves, and pray, and seek my face, and turn from their wicked ways: then will I hear from heaven, and will forgive their sin, and will heal their land!" May it be in our day.[317]

Where Do
We Go From Here?

Unto Him who is the author and giver
of all good, I render sincere and humble thanks
for His merciful and unmerited blessings,
and especially for our redemption and
salvation by his beloved Son.[318]

John Jay

The founding fathers had a great deal of wisdom. On balance, they were far more committed to the Christian faith than they are given credit for today. They showed us that there are many answers from the Bible and from history that are relevant for all time.

As our liberties continue to erode in modern America, I can't help but think of the words of our 4th president, James Madison: "Since the general civilization of mankind, I believe there are more instances of the abridgement of the freedom of the people by gradual and silent encroachments of those in power than by violent and sudden usurpations."[319] We need to heed these words.

Meanwhile, as Christians I believe strongly we should be committed to do what is right, regardless of how it turns out for us. We may win some, we may lose some. But I would rather fail trying to do the right thing than succeed in doing the wrong thing, every time.

A newspaper reporter asked me recently, "How has the conservative cause been going? There seem to have been a number of losses lately, like in economic policy and sexual morality and the new assertiveness of atheists." My remark to him was simple and to the point. "John Quincy Adams said, 'Duty is ours; results are God's.' That's our motto."[320]

Mother Teresa is reported to have said that God doesn't necessarily call us to be successful. But He does call us to be faithful. We should do what's right, as God gives us light to see what is right.

I do believe that the faith factor is one of the key missing components in modern people's understanding of the founding fathers. Again, not that all of them were committed Christians. But most of them were.

We need to make sure we do not miss out on something most of them enjoyed.

DON'T MISS OUT

John Jay was at the first Congress, co-wrote *The Federalist Papers,* and served as the first Chief Justice of the U.S. Supreme

Court. He said this: "By conveying the Bible to people...the Bible will also inform them, that our gracious Creator has provided for us a Redeemer, in whom all the nations of the earth should be blessed—that this Redeemer has made atonement "for the sins of the whole world," and thereby reconciling the Divine justice with the Divine mercy, has opened a way for our redemption and salvation; etc."[321]

Perhaps some readers don't understand the redemption he's talking about. It's as simple as ABC.

As we have seen, when many of the founding fathers, especially those from New England, learned their ABCs, they learned them from *The New England Primer,* which taught basic biblical principles along with the alphabet:

> A
> In Adam's Fall,
> We sinned all.
>
> B
> Thy life to mend,
> The Bible tend.
>
> C
> Christ crucify'd,
> For sinners died.

Because of Adam's sin, we are all sinners. Why was Christ crucified? God sent His Son, Jesus Christ, to conquer evil and to be the sacrifice needed to free us from the corrupting power of sin. Christ freed us and as liberated people, we become citizens of His kingdom and then live under His dominion for time and eternity. That was the view of the majority of the founders of this country, and it was a view that gave us liberty untold in the history of the world.

There is an ancient law proclaiming that only blood can atone for sin. People throughout all the centuries of human history, and in all kinds of different societies and cultures have known this. They have tried the blood of animals and of humans. They have tried and tried, but always come up short.

God saw our pitiful attempts and He had mercy on us. The blood of lambs and of bulls couldn't make us clean before God. So God Himself became the Lamb. That is what Christmas is all about—God becoming human. And God Himself became the sacrifice that was indeed good enough. That is what Easter is all about—Jesus dying on the cross to atone for our sins and rising from the dead three days later. That Cross became the bridge spanning the unassailable chasm between heaven and earth, between God and man.

The way to heaven is not closed any more. As the majority of the founders understood, now is the time of mercy. This is the time of grace. God freely offers us His salvation. He offers us the protection of His blood—good enough and clean enough for all eternity.

Some people think that we are saved by *doing* good works. But the truth is, rather, that we are saved *unto* good works. Good works are a natural by-product of a soul that is saved. Since the beginning of the Church, good works have followed the believers. Not only the keeping of the Ten Commandments, but acts of mercy. Jesus asked us to feed the hungry, clothe the naked, visit the prisoner, care for the sick and do good to strangers in His name. Christians do this in obedience to Jesus and in gratitude for our salvation. But in no way can good works make us right with God, because even our best work is contaminated by sin. However, if we confess our sins to God, which means simply that we agree with Him that they are wrong, He will forgive us.

So, if we turn away from our sins, and promise to try to stay away from sin, and with God's help, obey His commandments, then we have "repented." To be sorry for what we have done is the first step to getting right with God. The most important step is giving our life to God. If we give up the rights to our own life and give God the right to rule and decide, then we belong to Him—for time and eternity.

The words we use can be simple, like this:

Dear God, I know I'm not right with You. There are sins of many kinds in my life. I now turn away from them and forsake all evil. I ask you, Lord God, ruler of all, to take my life and rule it. Come in to my heart, Lord Jesus, and cleanse me and make me right with You. I acknowledge that You are the rightful God and Lord of the universe. Thank You for loving me and caring about me. Thank You for making me Yours and thank You that now I belong to You. In Jesus' name.

If you sincerely made these words your prayer or said a prayer like it, you are now a Christian. The Bible is your food, and prayer is your air, as a new creature of God. You need to tell somebody you know to be a Christian what you just did. And you need to find a church where you can be a part of the visible Church. I suggest you find a church where the Bible is preached and Christ is the focus.

I recommend that you write to Coral Ridge Ministries and request a book by Dr. D. James Kennedy, entitled *Beginning Again*. This book will help you understand more about what it means to be a Christian and to live the Christian life. The address is Truth in Action Ministries, Box 1, Ft. Lauderdale, FL 33302. God bless you as you do.

Soli Deo Gloria.

ACKNOWLEDGEMENTS

There are many people to thank for their help with this manuscript. Above all, Kirsti Newcombe, John Aman, Karen Gushta, and Nancy Britt provided excellent editing.

Many writers and speakers have had great influence in my understanding of our national Christian roots. Among these are Bill Federer, who was gracious enough to write a Foreword for this book, David Barton, Peter Lillback, Gary DeMar, Charles Hull Wolfe, Marshall Foster, and the late Peter Marshall.

Also, the late D. James Kennedy influenced my understanding probably more than anybody about the significant contribution of Christianity to the founding fathers in shaping their world-view. As the founder of Coral Ridge Ministries (now Truth in Action Ministries), he did so much to encourage us to see how the Bible and the Christian faith played such a vital role in the founding of our country.

ENDNOTES

1   Bruce Frohnen, ed., *The American Republic: Primary Sources* (Indianapolis: Liberty Fund, 2002), 189.

2   James Melvin Washington, ed., *A Testament of Hope: The Essential Writings of Martin Luther King, Jr.* (New York et al: Harper & Row, Publishers, 1986), 219.

3   Charles E. Kistler, *This Nation Under God* (Boston: Richard T. Badger, 1924), 73.

4   George Washington, "Farewell Address," September, 19, 1796, in *The Annals of America* (Chicago et al.: Encyclopaedia Britannica, 1976), 3:612.

5   Benjamin Hart, "The Wall That Protestantism Built: The Religious Reasons for the Separation of Church and State," *Policy Review*, Fall 1988, 44.

6   John Richard Green in his *History of the English People*, quoted in Verna Hall, ed., *The Christian History of the Constitution of the United States of America* (San Francisco: Foundation for American Christian Education, 1960/1993), 38.

7   Archbishop Steven Langton, The Magna Charta, quoted in Verna Hall, ed., *The Christian History of the Constitution of the United States of America* (San Francisco: Foundation for American Christian Education, 1960/1993), 38.

8   Joseph Reither, *World History at a Glance* (New York: The New Home Library, 1942), 184.

9   Quoted in Verna Hall, ed., *The Christian History of the Constitution of the United States of America* (San Francisco: Foundation for American Christian Education, 1960/1993), 2.

10   Ibid., 444.

11   George Bancroft, *History of the United States of America, From the Discovery of the Continent, Six Volumes* (New York: D. Appleton and Company, 1890), Vol. IV, 160.

12   Ibid.

13   Ibid.

14   Ibid.

15   Ibid.

16   Ibid., 393.

17   Ibid., 121.

18   Ibid., 420.

19   Ibid., 340.

20   Ibid., 274.

21   Mark A. Beliles' Introduction to an updated version of *Thomas Jefferson's Abridgement of The Words of Jesus of Nazareth* (Charlottesville, VA: The Providence Foundation, 1993), 11.

22   D. James Kennedy and Jerry Newcombe, *What If America Were a Christian Nation Again?* (Nashville: Thomas Nelson, Publishers, 2003), 54.

23   Bruce Frohnen, ed., The American Republic: Primary Sources (Indianapolis: Liberty Fund, 2002), 189-191.

24   John F. Kennedy, Inaugural Address, Jan. 20, 1961, in Caroline Thomas Harnsberger, ed., *Treasury of Presidential Quotations* (Chicago: Follett Publishing Company, 1964), 20.

25   Donald S. Lutz, *The Origins of American Constitutionalism,* (Baton Rouge: Louisiana State University Press, 1988), 115.

26   Quoted in Clinton Rossiter, *Seedtime of the Republic* (New York: Harcourt, Brace & World, Inc., 1953), 241.

27   Bruce Frohnen, ed., The American Republic: Primary Sources (Indianapolis: Liberty Fund, 2002), 190.

28   Donald S. Lutz, *The Origins of American Constitutionalism,* (Baton Rouge: Louisiana State University Press, 1988), 121.

29   *The Works of John Locke, A New Edition, Corrected In Ten Volumes* (London: Printed for

Thomas Tegg; W. Sharpe and Son, 1823, Reprinted 1963 by Scientia Verlag Aalen Germany), X:309.

30   Donald S. Lutz, *The Origins of American Constitutionalism,* (Baton Rouge: Louisiana State University Press, 1988), 68.

31   Ibid., 68, footnote 16.

32   Quoted in Hebert W. Titus, *God, Man, and Law: The Biblical Principles* (Oak Brook, IL: Institute in Basic Life Principles, 1994), 43.

33   Marshall Foster in D. James Kennedy, *One Nation Under God* (Ft. Lauderdale: Coral Ridge Ministries-TV, 2005), a video.

34   George Bancroft, *History of the United States of America, From the Discovery of the Continent,* Six Volumes (New York: D. Appleton and Company, 1890), Vol. IV, 383.

35   Ibid.

36   Ibid., 197.

37   Loraine Boettner, *The Reformed Doctrine of Predestination* (Philadelphia: The Presbyterian and Reformed Publishing Company, 1975), 387.

38   The Mecklenburgh Resolutions: May 20, 1775 (1) (2) The Avalon Project: Documents in Law, History and Diplomacy, Yale Law School, http://avalon.law.yale. edu/18th_century/nc06.asp

39   Bruce Frohnen, ed., The American Republic: Primary Sources (Indianapolis: Liberty Fund, 2002), 190-191.

40   N. S. McFetridge, *Calvinism in History,* 85-88, quoted in Loraine Boettner, *The Reformed Doctrine of Predestination* (Philadelphia: The Presbyterian and Reformed Publishing Company, 1975), 388.

41   Ibid., 442.

42   James Wilson, in his Lectures on Law, delivered at the College of Philadelphia in Charles Page Smith, *James Wilson: Founding Father* (Chapel Hill: University of North Carolina Press, 1956), 329.

43   John Adams to Thomas Jefferson, June 28th, 1813, in Lester J. Cappon, ed., *The Adams-Jefferson Letters: The Complete Correspondence Between Thomas Jefferson and Abigail and John Adams* (Chapel Hill, NC: the University of North Carolina Press, 1988), 338-340.

44   Ibid.

45   William J. Federer, *America's God and Country* (St. Louis: Amerisearch, 2000), 530.

46   George Washington, "First Inaugural Address," April 30, 1789, in John Rhodehamel, ed., *George Washington: Writings* (New York: The Library of America, 1997), 731-732.

47   Transcript of an interview with Stephen McDowell by Jerry Newcombe (Ft. Lauderdale: Truth in Action Ministries, 2011).

48   George Washington, "First Inaugural Address," April 30, 1789, in John Rhodehamel, ed., *George Washington: Writings* (New York: The Library of America, 1997), 731-732.

49   Transcript of an interview with Stephen McDowell by Jerry Newcombe (Ft. Lauderdale: Truth in Action Ministries, 2011).

50   Abraham Lincoln, "Proclamation for a National Day of Fasting," March 30, 1863, in Marion Mills Miller, ed., *Life and Works of Abraham Lincoln Centenary Edition.* In Nine Volumes (New York: The Current Literature Publishing Co., 1907), VI, 156.

51   John Eidsmoe, *Christianity and the Constitution - The Faith of Our Founding Fathers* (Grand Rapids, MI: Baker Book House, 1987), 146.

52   Andrew Jackson, June 8, 1845, in Henry Halley, *Halley's Bible Handbook* (Grand Rapids, MI: Zondervan, 1927, 1965), 18.

53   Ulysses S. Grant, June 6, 1876, in a letter from Washington during his term as President, to the Editor of the *Sunday School Times* in Philadelphia. Stephen Abbott Northrop, *A Cloud of Witnesses* (Portland, OR: American Heritage Ministries, 1987), 195.

54   William J. Federer, *America's God and Country: Encyclopedia of Quotations* (St. Louis, MO: Amerisearch, 2000), 246.

55   Saxe Commins, ed., *The Basic Writings of George Washington* (NY: Random House, 1948), 410.

56   John C. Fitzpatrick, ed., *The Writings of Washington*, Vol. XII, (Washington, D.C.: U.S. Government Printing Office, 1932), 343.

57   Jonathan Trumbull quoted in Hezekiah Niles, *Principles and Acts of the Revolution in America* (Baltimore: William Ogden Niles, 1822), 198.

58   George Bancroft, *History of the United States of America, From the Discovery of the Continent*, Six Volumes (New York: D. Appleton and Company, 1890), Vol. IV, 22.

59   Ibid., 72.

60   Ibid.

61   Ibid., 25.

62   Ibid., 20.

63   William J. Federer, *America's God and Country: Encyclopedia of Quotations* (St. Louis, MO: Amerisearch, 2000), 637.

64   Ibid., 73.

65   William Prescott, quoted in Lucille Johnston, *Celebrations of a Nation* (Arlington, VA: The Year of Thanksgiving Foundation, 1987), 76.

66   George Bancroft, *History of the United States of America, From the Discovery of the Continent*, Six Volumes (New York: D. Appleton and Company, 1890), Vol. IV, 20.

67   Ibid., 45.

68   Stephen J. Keillor, *This Rebellious House* (Downers Grove, IL: IVP, 1996), 89.

69   George Bancroft, *History of the United States of America, From the Discovery of the Continent*, Six Volumes (New York: D. Appleton and Company, 1890), Vol. IV, 341.

70   Ibid., 43-44.

71   Ibid., 44.

72   Ibid., 65.

73   Ibid., 46.

74   Ibid., 54.

75   Ibid., 92.

76   Frank S. Mead, *The Encyclopedia of Religious Quotations* (Old Tappan, NJ: Fleming H. Revell Company, 1965), 150.

77   Declaration of Independence, Bruce Frohnen, ed., *The American Republic: Primary Sources* (Indianapolis: Liberty Fund, 2002), 190.

78   George Bancroft, *History of the United States of America, From the Discovery of the Continent*, Six Volumes (New York: D. Appleton and Company, 1890), Vol. IV, 21.

79   Ibid., 57.

80   Ibid., 330.

81   Ibid., 75.

82   Ibid., 76.

83   Ibid., 76.

84   Ibid., 74.

85   Frank S. Mead, *The Encyclopedia of Religious Quotations* (Old Tappan, NJ: Fleming H. Revell Company, 1965), 153.

86   George Bancroft, *History of the United States of America, From the Discovery of the Continent*, Six Volumes (New York: D. Appleton and Company, 1890), Vol. IV, 72.

87   Ibid., 72.

88   Ibid., 93.

89   Ibid., 138.

90   Ibid., 123.

91   Frank S. Mead, *The Encyclopedia of Religious Quotations* (Old Tappan, NJ: Fleming H. Revell Company, 1965), 153.

92   George Bancroft, *History of the United States of America, From the Discovery of the Continent*, Six Volumes (New York: D. Appleton and Company, 1890), Vol. IV, 426.

93   Ibid., 172.

94   Ibid., 231.

95   Ibid., 103.

96   Ibid., 118.

97   Ibid., 130.

98   Ibid., 231.

99   Ibid., 112.

100   Ibid., 113.

101   Quoted in Stephen Abbott Northrop, *A Cloud of Witnesses* (Portland, OR: American Heritage Ministries, 1987) 208.

102   George Bancroft, *History of the United States of America, From the Discovery of the Continent,* Six Volumes (New York: D. Appleton and Company, 1890), Vol. IV, 113.

103   Ibid., 205.

104   Ibid., 238.

105   Ibid., 199.

106   James Russel Lowell, "Once to Every Man and Nation," *The HYMNAL for Worship & Celebration* (Nashville: Word Music, 1986), Hymn #475.

107   Benjamin Rush, "A Plan for the Establishment of Public Schools and the Diffusion of Knowledge in Pennsylvania; to Which Are Added, Thoughts upon the Mode of Education, Proper in a Republic" 1786, reprinted in Charles S. Hyneman, Donald S. Lutz, *AMERICAN Political Writing during the Founding Era 1760-1805, Volume I* (Indianapolis: Liberty Fund, 1983), 681.

108   Benjamin Rush, "A Defence of the Use of the Bible in Schools," a tract from the 1830s, http://www.biblebelievers.com/Bible_in_schools.html.

109   Second Annual Message to Congress, Dec. 5, 1810, Caroline Thomas Harnsberger, ed., *Treasury of Presidential Quotations* (Chicago: Follett Publishing Company, 1964), 75.

110   George Washington, "Farewell Address," 1796, *The Annals of America* (Chicago et al.: Encyclopaedia Britannica, 1976), Vol. 3, 612.

111   Patrick Henry, "Provision for Teachers of the Christian Religion" (1784) in Anson Phelps Stokes and Leo Pfeffer, *Church and State in the United States,* Three Volumes (NY: Harper & Brothers, Publishers, 1955), 97-98.

112   June 2, 1778, in a diary entry made while in Paris, France. L.H. Butterfield, ed., *Diary and Autobiography of John Adams* (Cambridge, MA: Belknap Press of Harvard University Press, 1961), Vol. IV, 123.

113   *The New-England Primer* (Boston: Edward Draper's Printing-Office, 1690/1777. Reprinted by David Barton (Aledo, TX: Wallbuilders, 1991), the pages are unnumbered.

114   Transcript of an interview with Rick Green by Jerry Newcombe on location in Aledo, TX (Ft. Lauderdale: Coral Ridge Ministries, 2005).

115   Transcript of an interview with Donald S. Lutz by Jerry Newcombe on location in Houston (Ft. Lauderdale: Coral Ridge Ministries, 2005).

116   "New England's First Fruits," 1643, quoted in *The Annals of America* (Chicago et al.: Encyclopaedia Britannica, 1976), Vol. 1, 175.

117   Rules for Harvard University, 1643, from "New England's First Fruits," *The Annals of America* (Chicago et al.: Encyclopaedia Britannica, 1976), Vol. 1, 176 (emphasis in original).

118   "The Statutes of the College of William and Mary," *The Annals of America* (Chicago et al.: Encyclopaedia Britannica, 1976), Vol. 1, 371.

119   "Regulations at Yale College," 1745, *The Annals of America* (Chicago et al.: Encyclopaedia Britannica, 1976), Vol. 1, 464.

120   Quoted in Paul Lee Tan, *Encyclopedia of 7,700 Illustrations: Signs of the Times* (Rockville, MD: Assurance Publishers, 1984), 158.

121   Stephen K. McDowell and Mark A. Beliles, *America's Providential History* (Charlottesville, VA: Providence Press, 1988), 93.

122   William J. Federer, *America's God and Country: Encyclopedia of Quotations* (St. Louis, MO: Amerisearch, 2000), 520.

123   Article III of "The Northwest Ordinance," the United States Congress, adopted 1787 and re-adopted 1789, in *The Annals of America* (Chicago et al.: Encyclopaedia Britannica,

1976), Vol. 3, 194-195.

124 Quoted in Gary DeMar, *America's Christian History: The Untold Story* (Atlanta, American Vision, Publishers, 1993), 22.

125 Woodrow Wilson, remarks at a Denver rally, 1911 in Charles E. Rice, *The Supreme Court and Public Prayer.* New York: Fordham University Press, 1964, 61-62.

126 Transcript of a TV interview with William J. Murray by Jerry Newcombe (Ft. Lauderdale: Coral Ridge Ministries, 1996).

127 Transcript of a TV interview with Ann Coulter by Jerry Newcombe on location in New York City (Ft. Lauderdale: Coral Ridge Ministries, 2006).

128 William J. Federer's "American Quotations," in William J. Federer, ed., *Library of Classics* (St. Louis, MO: Amerisearch, Inc., 2002), a CD-ROM.

129 George Washington, May 10, 1789, *The Writings of Washington,* Vol. XXX, 32.

130 John Witherspoon in Roger Schultz, "Covenanting in America: The Political Theology of John Witherspoon," Master's Thesis, Trinity Evangelical Divinity School, Deerfield, Illinois, 1985, pp. 113, 124. John Eidsmoe, *Christianity and The Constitution - The Faith of Our Founding Fathers* (Grand Rapids, MI: Baker Book House, A Mott Media Book, 1987, 6th printing 1993), 90-91.

131 *Runkel v. Winemiller,* 4 Harris & McHenry 276, 288 (Sup. Ct. Md. 1799).

132 George Bancroft, *History of the United States of America, From the Discovery of the Continent,* Six Volumes (New York: D. Appleton and Company, 1890), Vol. IV, 416.

133 Ibid., 417.

134 Annual Message to Congress, 6 Jan. 1941; *Public Papers, IX,* 672 in Caroline Thomas Harnsberger, ed., *Treasury of Presidential Quotations* (Chicago: Follett Publishing Company, 1964), 108-109.

135 Ibid.

136 Transcript of a TV interview of Chief Justice Roy Moore by Jerry Newcombe on location in Montgomery, Alabama (Ft. Lauderdale: Coral Ridge Ministries, 2003).

137 Transcript of a TV interview of Ira Glasser by Jerry Newcombe (Ft. Lauderdale: Coral Ridge Ministries, 1991).

138 Bruce Frohnen, ed., *The American Republic: Primary Sources* (Indianapolis: Liberty Fund, 2002), 327.

139 Ibid., 328.

140 Alexis de Tocqueville, *The Republic of the United States of America and Its Political Institutions,* Reviewed and Examined, trans. Paul Reeves, (Garden City, NY: A.S. Barnes and Co., 1851), Vol. 1, 337.

141 *Church of the Holy Trinity v. the United States.* No. 143. Supreme Court of the United States

142 U.S. 457 36 L.Ed. 226, 12 S.Ct. 511, 29 February, 1892. Decided.

143 Larry Witham, "'Christian Nation' Now Fighting Words," *The Washington Times,* November 23, 1992, A1.

144 Robert Cord, *Separation of Church and State: Historical Fact and Current Fiction* (New York: Lambeth Press, 1982), 4.

145 Robert Cord, *Separation of Church and State: Historical Fact and Current Fiction* (New York: Lambeth Press, 1982), 7.

146 Saul K. Padover, *The Complete Madison* (New York: Harper and Brothers, 1953), 306.

147 Robert Cord, *Separation of Church and State: Historical Fact and Current Fiction* (New York: Lambeth Press, 1982), 15.

148 David Barton, *Original Intent* (Aledo, TX: Wallbuilders, 1996), 156.

149 *Time* Magazine, December 9, 1991, 64.

150 "The Supreme Court," *Time* Magazine, Vol. LXXX, No. 1, July 6, 1962, 7.

151 "While Most Believe in God..." *Newsweek,* July 9, 1962, 44.

152 Ibid.

153 Justice William Rehnquist, Dissenting Opinion, *Wallace v. Jaffree,* 1985, http://www.law.cornell.edu/supct/html/historics/USSC_CR_0472_0038_ZD2.html

154 Transcript of a TV interview with Sen. James Inhofe by Jerry Newcombe on location in

Washington, D.C. (Ft. Lauderdale: Coral Ridge Ministries, 2010).

155   Reports of Committees of the House of Represenatives Made During the First Session of the Thirty-Third Congress (Washington: A. O. P. Nicholson, 1854). p.6.

156   John Adams, October 11, 1798, in a letter to the officers of the First Brigade of the Third Division of the Militia of Massachusetts. Charles Francis Adams (son of John Quincy Adams and grandson of John Adams), ed., *The Works of John Adams - Second President of the United States: with a Life of the Author, Notes, and Illustration* (Boston: Little, Brown, & Co., 1854), Vol. IX, 228-229.

157   Ibid.

158   Benjamin Hart, "The Wall That Protestantism Built: The Religious Reasons for the Separation of Church and State," *Policy Review*, Fall 1988, 44.

159   John Eidsmoe, *Christianity and the Constitution* (Grand Rapids: Baker Book House), 51.

160   David Barton, in D. James Kennedy, *What if Jesus Had Never Been Born?* (Ft. Lauderdale, FL: Coral Ridge Ministries-TV, December 25, 2002), a television special.

161   Baron Charles Montesquieu, *The Spirit of the Laws*, 1748, Anne Cohler, trans. (Cambridge: Cambridge University Press, 1989), 457.

162   Ibid.

163   Rosie O'Donnell, *The View*, ABC-TV, September 12, 2006.

164   Chief Justice Roy S. Moore, *Our Legal Heritage* (Montgomery, AL: The Administrative Office of Courts, June 2001), 8.

165   Sir William Blackstone, *Commentaries on the Laws of England*, 4 Volumes (Philadelphia: J. B. Lippincott and Co., 1879), Vol. I, 39, 41, 42.

166   Ibid.

167   Quoted in Hebert W. Titus, *God, Man, and Law: The Biblical Principles* (Oak Brook, IL: Institute in Basic Life Principles, 1994), 44.

168   John Locke, *The Second Treatise Of Civil Government*, 1690 (Buffalo, NY: Prometheus Books, 1986) 77.

169   Thomas Jefferson to William Canby, 18 September 1813, Writings, XIII:377. Quoted in Caroline Thomas Harnsberger, ed., *Treasury of Presidential Quotations* (Chicago: Follett Publishing Company, 1964), 194.

170   Donald S. Lutz, *The Origins of American Constitutionalism*, (Baton Rouge: Louisiana State University Press, 1988), 28.

171   Ibid., 28.

172   Ibid., 85 [emphasis his].

173   Ibid., 83.

174   Ibid., 86.

175   Albert Henry Smyth, ed., *The Writings of Benjamin Franklin*, 10 vols. (New York: Macmillan Co., 1905-7), Vol. 9, 569.

176   Donald S. Lutz, *The Origins of American Constitutionalism*, (Baton Rouge: Louisiana State University Press, 1988), 86.

177   Ibid., 87.

178   Benjamin Franklin, "Readings for Americans - Articles of Lasting Interest" (Pleasantville, N.Y.: Reader's Digest, The Reader's Digest Association, Inc.), 106.

179   William S. Pfaff, ed., *Maxims and Morals of Benjamin Franklin* (New Orleans: Searcy and Pfaff, Ltd., 1927).

180   Benjamin Franklin, January 1, 1769, in a letter to Lord James. Paul W. Connor, *Poor Richard's Politiks – Benjamin Franklin and His American Order* (NY: Oxford University Press, 1965), 107.

181   Abraham Lincoln, "Remarks upon the Holy Scriptures, in Receiving the Present of a Bible from a Negro Delegation," September 7, 1864, Marion Mills Miller, ed., *Life and Works of Abraham Lincoln: Centenary Edition*, In Nine Volumes (New York: The Current Literature Publishing Co., 1907), Vol. V, 209.

182   John Eidsmoe, *Christianity and the Constitution* (Grand Rapids: Baker Book House, 1987), 188.

183   Fyodor Dostoevsky, Andrew H. MacAndrew, trans., *The Brothers Karamazov* (Toronto, et al: Bantam Books, 1970), Book XI, Chapter 8, 760.

184   Martin Luther King, Jr., February, 1964, *The Wisdom of Martin Luther King In His Own Words* (New York: Lancer Books, 1968), 106.

185   Robert Charles Winthrop, Remarks to the Massachusetts Bible Society, Boston, May 28, 1849, in *Addresses and Speeches on Various Occasions* (Boston: Little, Brown & Company, 1852), 172.

186   George Washington, "Circular to State Governments," June 8, 1783, in John Rhodehamel, ed., *George Washington: Writings* (New York: The Library of America, 1997), 526.

187   Ibid.

188   George Washington, *Writings* (1932), Vol. XV, 55, from his speech to the Delaware Indian Chiefs on May 12, 1779, quoted in David Barton, *Original Intent* (Aledo, TX: Wallbuilders, 1996), 168.

189   William J. Murray, *My Life Without God* (Nashville: Thomas Nelson, 1982), 14.

190   Ibid., 232-233. [emphasis his]

191   Transcript of a Coral Ridge Ministries television interview with William J. Murray, conducted by Jerry Newcombe, on location in Dallas, May 24, 1989.

192   November 20, 1798, a Certified Copy of "Last Will and Testament of Patrick Henry," Patrick Henry Memorial Foundation, Red Hill, Brookneal, Virginia, in Henry, ed., *Patrick Henry - Life, Correspondence and Speeches*, Vol. II, 631, as quoted in William J. Federer's "American Quotations," in William J. Federer, ed., *Library of Classics* (St. Louis, MO: Amerisearch, Inc., 2002), a CD-ROM.

193   Letter from Cal Thomas to Jerry Newcombe, April 15, 1995.

194   John Adams in a letter to Thomas Jefferson, December 25, 1813, in Norman Cousins, *In God We Trust - The Religious Beliefs and Ideas of the American Founding Fathers* (NY: Harper & Brothers, 1958), 256.

195   Ashabel Green, *The Life of the Rev. John Witherspoon* (Princeton: Princeton University Press, reprinted 1973, 173.

196   To William Canby, Sept. 18, 1813, *Writings, XIII*, 377 in Caroline Thomas Harnsberger, ed., *Treasury of Presidential Quotations* (Chicago: Follett Publishing Company, 1964), 194.

197   George Bancroft, *History of the United States of America, From the Discovery of the Continent*, Six Volumes (New York: D. Appleton and Company, 1890), Vol. IV, 433.

198   Ibid., 432.

199   Ibid., 59.

200   Andrew Johnson, Speech in Washington, D.C., 22 February 1866; *Document*, 4, in Caroline Thomas Harnsberger, ed., *Treasury of Presidential Quotations* (Chicago: Follett Publishing Company, 1964), 128.

201   Theodore Roosevelt, 1916; *Works, XVIII*, 199 in Caroline Thomas Harnsberger, ed., *Treasury of Presidential Quotations* (Chicago: Follett Publishing Company, 1964), 117.

202   President Harry Truman, News Conference, April 6, 1946 in Caroline Thomas Harnsberger, ed., *Treasury of Presidential Quotations* (Chicago: Follett Publishing Company, 1964), 195.

203   George Washington, October 3, 1789, in Jared Sparks, ed., *The Writings of George Washington*, 12 vols. (Boston: American Stationer's Company, 1837, NY: F. Andrew's, 1834-1847), Vol. XII, 119 [emphasis mine].

204   John Jay, October 12, 1816, in Henry P. Johnston, ed., *The Correspondence and Public Papers of John Jay* (New York: Burt Franklin, 1970), Vol. 4, 393.

205   William Jay, The Life of John Jay, Vol. 1 (New York: J. and J. Harper, 1833), 70.

206   Abraham Kuyper, *You Can Do Greater Things Than Christ*, trans. Jan H. Boer (Jos, Nigeria: Institute of Church and Society, 1991), 74. This comes from the first volume of Kuyper's book, which was first published as *Pro Rege, of Het Koningschap van Christus* in 1911.

207   D. James Kennedy, "A Christian Offensive," (Ft. Lauderdale: Coral Ridge Ministries, 1980).

208   Caroline Thomas Harnsberger, ed., *Treasury of Presidential Quotations* (Chicago: Follett Publishing Company, 1964), 117.

209   John Newton, quoted in Charles W. Colson, "Standing tough against all odds: His 40-year struggle against slavery makes William Wilberforce a model of Christian persistence," *Christianity Today*, September 6, 1985, 27.

210   William Pitt, quoted in Basil Miller, *10 Handicapped Boys and Girls who became Famous*, 29.

211   John Wesley letter to Wilberforce, 1791, quoted in Travers Buxton, *William Wilberforce: The Story of a Great Crusade* (London: The Religious Tract Society, undated), 80.

212   Charles W. Colson, "Standing tough against all odds: His 40-year struggle against slavery makes William Wilberforce a model of Christian persistence," *Christianity Today*, September 6, 1985, 27.

213   D. James Kennedy with Jerry Newcombe, *The Gates of Hell Shall Not Prevail* (Nashville: Thomas Nelson Publishers, 1996), 199-201, 233-235.

214   Abraham Lincoln, December 10, 1856, in Marion Mills Miller, ed., *Life and Works of Abraham Lincoln Centenary Edition*. In Nine Volumes (New York: The Current Literature Publishing Co., 1907), Vol. 3, 10.

215   Abraham Lincoln, First Inaugural Address, 4 March 1861, Caroline Thomas Harnsberger, ed., *Treasury of Presidential Quotations* (Chicago: Follett Publishing Company, 1964), 127.

216   Andrew Johnson, To soldiers in camp, 1862; *Not Guilty*, 68, in Caroline Thomas Harnsberger, ed., *Treasury of Presidential Quotations* (Chicago: Follett Publishing Company, 1964), 127.

217   Theodore Roosevelt, Fifth Annual Message to Congress, 5 December 1905, *Messages and Papers*, 7366, in Caroline Thomas Harnsberger, ed., *Treasury of Presidential Quotations* (Chicago: Follett Publishing Company, 1964), 129.

218   Theodore Roosevelt, Speech at Asheville, N.C., 9 September 1902; *Dictionary*, 486, in Caroline Thomas Harnsberger, ed., *Treasury of Presidential Quotations* (Chicago: Follett Publishing Company, 1964), 129.

219   Theodore Roosevelt, Speech at St. Louis, Mo., 28 March 1912; *Works, XVII*, 173, in Caroline Thomas Harnsberger, ed., *Treasury of Presidential Quotations* (Chicago: Follett Publishing Company, 1964), 129.

220   Alexander Hamilton, James Madison, and John Jay, *The Federalist Papers*, introduction by Clinton Rossiter (New York, et al.: A Mentor Book from New American Library, 1961), 322.

221   Thomas Jefferson, Letter to Joseph C. Cabell, 2 Feb. 1816; *Works, VI*, 541, Caroline Thomas Harnsberger, ed., *Treasury of Presidential Quotations* (Chicago: Follett Publishing Company, 1964), 122.

222   Martha Lou Lemmon Stohlman, *John Witherspoon: Parson, Politician, Patriot* (Philadelphia: Westminster Press, 1897), 101-102.

223   Roger Schultz, "Covenanting in America: The Political Theology of John Witherspoon," Master's Thesis, Trinity Evangelical Divinity School, Deerfield, Illinois, 1985, pp. 136-137.

224   John Eidsmoe, *Christianity and The Constitution - The Faith of Our Founding Fathers* (Grand Rapids, MI: Baker Book House, A Mott Media Book, 1987, 6th printing 1993), 88.

225   M. E. Bradford, *A Worthy Company* (Marlborough, NH: Plymouth Rock Foundation, 1982), 147.

226   Articles of Confederation, 1778, in Bruce Frohnen, ed., *The American Republic: Primary Sources* (Indianapolis: Liberty Fund, 2002), 204.

227   Alexander Hamilton, James Madison, and John Jay, *The Federalist Papers*, introduction by Clinton Rossiter (New York, et al.: A Mentor Book from New American Library, 1961) xi.

228   Ibid., 80.

229   Alexander Hamilton, James Madison, and John Jay, *The Federalist Papers*, introduction by Clinton Rossiter (New York, et al.: A Mentor Book from New American Library, 1961) 301.

230	John Eidsmoe, *Christianity and the Constitution: The Faith of our Founding Fathers* (Grand Rapids, MI: Baker Book House, 1987), 101.
231	Ibid., 89.
232	Alexander Hamilton, James Madison, and John Jay, *The Federalist Papers*, introduction by Clinton Rossiter (New York, et al.: A Mentor Book from New American Library, 1961), 322.
233	Ibid., 346.
234	Ibid., 59.
235	Ibid., 110.
236	Quoted in Catherine Drinker Bowen, *Miracle at Philadelphia: The Story of the Constitutional Convention May to September 1787* (Boston et al.: An Atlantic Monthly Press Book, a division of Little, Brown and Company, 1966/1986), 61.
237	John Eidsmoe, *Christianity and the Constitution* (Grand Rapids: Baker Book House, 1987), 428.
238	Catherine Drinker Bowen, *Miracle at Philadelphia: The Story of the Constitutional Convention May to September 1787* (Boston et al.: An Atlantic Monthly Press Book, a division of Little, Brown and Company, 1966 / 1986), 138.
239	George Washington, letter to Henry Lee, October 31, 1786, *Writings* (Fitzpatrick), XXIX, 33 in Caroline Thomas Harnsberger, ed., *Treasury of Presidential Quotations* (Chicago: Follett Publishing Company, 1964), 186.
240	Peggy Lamson, *Roger Baldwin: Founder of the American Civil Liberties Union* (Boston, MA: Houghton Mifflin Company, 1976), 64.
241	D. James Kennedy and Jerry Newcombe, *Lord of All: Developing a Christian World-and-Life View* (Wheaton, IL: Crossway Books, 2005), 126.
242	David C. Gibbs, Jr. with Jerry Newcombe, *One Nation Under God: Ten Things Every Christian Should Know About the Founding of America* (Seminole, FL: Christian Law Association, 2003), 147.
243	Rev. John Witherspoon, "The Dominion of Providence Over the Passions of Men," May 17, 1775, at *TeachingAmericanHistory.org*
244	Ibid.
245	George Bancroft, *History of the United States of America, From the Discovery of the Continent*, Six Volumes (New York: D. Appleton and Company, 1890), Vol. IV, 431.
246	Ibid., 241.
247	Ibid.
248	Ibid., 263.
249	Ibid., 341.
250	Ibid., 441.
251	Letter to Elbridge Gerry, January 29, 1780, Carol Kelly-Gangi, ed., *The Essential Wisdom of the Founding Fathers* (New York: Fall River Press, 2009), 82.
252	George Bancroft, *History of the United States of America, From the Discovery of the Continent*, Six Volumes (New York: D. Appleton and Company, 1890), Vol. IV, 425.
253	Ibid., 77.
254	Ibid., 132.
255	Ibid., 94.
256	Ibid., 396.
257	Ibid., 438.
258	Ibid., 440.
259	Ibid., 355.
260	Bruce Frohnen, ed., *The American Republic: Primary Sources* (Indianapolis: Liberty Fund, 2002), 190.
261	George Bancroft, *History of the United States of America, From the Discovery of the Continent*, Six Volumes (New York: D. Appleton and Company, 1890), Vol. IV, 125.
262	Ibid., 125.
263	Patrick Henry, quoted in "Marvelous Bible Quotes," at *BibleResources.org*.

264   George Bancroft, *History of the United States of America, From the Discovery of the Continent*, Six Volumes (New York: D. Appleton and Company, 1890), Vol. IV, 180.

265   Ibid., 145.

266   *The Annals of America*, 20 vols. (Chicago, IL: Encyclopedia Britannica, 1968), Vol. 2, 322-333.

267   William J. Federer, *America's God and Country: Encyclopedia of Quotations* (St. Louis, MO: Amerisearch, 2000), 330.

268   Ibid., 330.

269   Thomas Jefferson, September 28, 1820, in a letter to William Jarvis, in Wilson Whitman, ed., *Jefferson's Letters* (Eau Claire, WI: E.M. Hale & Co., 1900), 338.

270   Alexander Hamilton, James Madison, and John Jay, *The Federalist Papers*, with introduction by Clinton Rossiter (New York, et al.: A Mentor Book from New American Library, 1961), 316.

271   Ibid.

272   Montesquieu, "Spirit of Laws." vol. i., page 186. Alexander Hamilton, James Madison, and John Jay, *The Federalist Papers*, with introduction by Clinton Rossiter (New York, et al.: A Mentor Book from New American Library, 1961), 466.

273   Alexander Hamilton, James Madison, and John Jay, *The Federalist Papers*, with introduction by Clinton Rossiter (New York, et al.: A Mentor Book from New American Library, 1961), 467.

274   Transcript from a Coral Ridge Ministries-TV interview with George Grant by Jerry Newcombe (Ft. Lauderdale: Coral Ridge Ministries, 1998).

275   Transcript from a Coral Ridge Ministries-TV interview with Jay Sekulow by Jerry Newcombe (Ft. Lauderdale: Coral Ridge Ministries, 2006).

276   John-Henry Westen and Gudrun Schultz "Canadian City Councillor Fined $1000 for Saying Homosexuality 'not Normal or Natural'" LifeSiteNews.com, January 18, 2007.

277   Stephane Courtois, et al, *The Black Book of Communism: Crimes, Terror, Repression* (Cambridge, MA: Harvard University Press, 1999).

278   *Stone v. Graham*, 449 U.S. 39 (1980). www.supremecourtus.gov/opinions

279   Abraham Lincoln, "First Inaugural Address," March 4, 1861, in *The Annals of America* (Chicago et al.: Encyclopaedia Britannica, 1976), Vol. 9, 254.

280   Alexander Hamilton, James Madison, and John Jay, *The Federalist Papers*, with introduction by Clinton Rossiter (New York, et al.: A Mentor Book from New American Library, 1961), 211-217.

281   John Adams to Abigail Adams, 26 April 1777, Familiar Letters, 265. Quoted in Caroline Thomas Harnsberger, ed., *Treasury of Presidential Quotations* (Chicago: Follett Publishing Company, 1964), 106.

282   William Vincent Wells, *The Life And Public Services Of Samuel Adams: being a narrative of his acts*, Vol. 4 (Boston: Little, Brown & Company, 1865) p. 415.

283   George Washington, "Farewell Address," September, 19, 1796, in *The Annals of America* (Chicago et al.: Encyclopaedia Britannica, 1976), Vol. 3, 612.

284   Thomas Jefferson, First Inaugural Address, March 4, 1801, in Carol Kelly-Gangi, ed., *The Essential Wisdom of the Founding Fathers* (New York: Fall River Press, 2009), 45.

285   Thomas Jefferson in a letter to Elbridge Gerry, January 26, 1799; *Works, IV,* 268 in Caroline Thomas Harnsberger, ed., *Treasury of Presidential Quotations* (Chicago: Follett Publishing Company, 1964), 53.

286   James Madison in a letter to Henry Lee, April 13, 1790, *Complete Madison*, 336 in Caroline Thomas Harnsberger, ed., *Treasury of Presidential Quotations* (Chicago: Follett Publishing Company, 1964), 53.

287   No one knows for sure the exact source of this quote. An exhaustive search through the writings of Alexis de Tocqueville, one of those to whom this is commonly attributed yields no results. Sometimes this quote is attributed to Alexander Tytler, who later became Lord Alexander Fraser Woodhouselee, in his book *The Decline and Fall of the Athenian Republic*. One Internet source lists the quote this way: "A democracy can not

exist as a permanent form of government. It can only exist until the voters discover that they can vote themselves largesse from the Public Treasury . . . with the result that a democracy always collapses over loose fiscal policy." Source: http://www.freedonia.org/spectre.html

288   Samuel Adams, "The Rights of the Colonists" (Boston: Old South Leaflets, 1772), Vol. VII. Selim H. Peabody, ed., *American Patriotism - Speeches, Letters, and Other Papers Which Illustrate the Foundation, the Development, the Preservation of the United States of America* (NY: American Book Exchange, 1880), 34.

289   Martin Luther King, Jr., "Love, Law, and Civil Disobedience," November 16, 1961, in James Melvin Washington, ed., *A Testament of Hope: The Essential Writings of Martin Luther King, Jr.* (New York et al: Harper & Row, Publishers, 1986), 50.

290   Transcript from a TV interview of Congressman Allen West by Jerry Newcombe (Ft. Lauderdale: Coral Ridge Ministries, 2010).

291   Ibid.

292   Ibid.

293   Transcript from a TV interview of Congressman Mike McIntyre on location in Washington, D.C., by Jerry Newcombe (Ft. Lauderdale: Coral Ridge Ministries, 2010).

294   D. James Kennedy and Jerry Newcombe, *How Would Jesus Vote? A Christian Perspective on the Issues* (Colorado Springs: WaterBrook, 2008), 110-111.

295   Ibid., 118.

296   Joshua Muravchik, *Heaven on Earth: The Rise and Fall of Socialism* (San Francisco: Encounter Books, 2002), 321.

297   Transcript from a TV interview of Congressman Michele Bachmann on location in Washington, D.C. by Jerry Newcombe (Ft. Lauderdale: Coral Ridge Ministries, 2010).

298   Transcript from a TV interview of Congressman Mike Pence on location in Washington, D.C. by Jerry Newcombe (Ft. Lauderdale: Coral Ridge Ministries, 2010).

299   Katrina Trinko, "Obama: Not Always a Fan of Upping Debt Ceiling," January 3, 2011, http://www.nationalreview.com/corner/256199/obama-not-always-fan-upping-debt-ceiling-katrina-trinko.

300   Transcript from a TV interview of Bill Federer by Jerry Newcombe (Ft. Lauderdale: Coral Ridge Ministries, 2010).

301   William J. Federer, *America's God and Country* (St. Louis: Amerisearch, 2000), 248.

302   Robert Flood, *The Men Who Shaped America* (Chicago: Moody Press, 1976), 51-52.

303   Benjamin Franklin, *The Autobiography of Benjamin Franklin: Poor Richard's Almanac and Other Papers* (Reading, PA: The Spencer Press, 1936), Franklin, *Autobiography*, 133.

304   Paul Johnson, *A History of the American People* (New York: HarperCollinsPublishers, 1997), 115.

305   Ibid., 116.

306   Ibid., 116-117.

307   Ibid.

308   John Hancock, April 15, 1775, Massachusetts Provincial Congress declaring a Day of Public Humiliation, Fasting and Prayer. Proclamation of John Hancock from Concord (from an original in the Evans collection, #14220, by the American Antiquarian Society. William Lincoln, ed., The Journals of Each Provincial Congress of Massachusetts, 1774-1775 (Boston: Dutton & Wentworth, 1838), 114-145 in William J. Federer, *America's God and Country: Encyclopedia of Quotations* (St. Louis, MO: Amerisearch, 2000), 275-276.

309   Jonathan Trumbull, April 19, 1775, as Governor of the Connecticut Colony proclaiming a day of fasting and prayer. Verna M. Hall, *The Christian History of the American Revolution* (San Francisco: Foundation for American Christian Education, 1976), 407.

310   Benjamin Franklin, 28 June 1787. James Madison, *Notes of Debates in the Federal Convention of 1787.* Gaillard Hunt and James B. Scott, ed., *The Debates in the Federal Convention of 1787 Which Framed the Constitution of the United States of America, reported by James Madison* (New York: Oxford University Press, 1920), 181-182.

311   E.C. M'Guire, *The Religious Opinions and Character of Washington* (NY: Harper & Brothers,

1836), 151.

312 John Eidsmoe, *Christianity and the Constitution* (Grand Rapids: Baker Book House, 1987), 209.

313 Benjamin Franklin, 28 June 1787. James Madison, *Notes of Debates in the Federal Convention of 1787* (New York: W.W. Norton & Co., 1787/1987), 210-211.

314 M'Guire, *The Religious Opinions and Character of Washington*, 152, as quoted in William J. Federer, *America's God and Country: Encyclopedia of Quotations* (St. Louis, MO: Amerisearch, 2000), 249.

315 John Hancock, October 5, 1791 Thanksgiving proclamation, issued while he was Governor of Massachusetts; as printed in the Columbian Centinel, October 15, 1791.

316 *The Annals of America* (Chicago et al.: *Encyclopedia Britannica*, 1976), Vol. 3, 345.

317 D. James Kennedy, *What If America Were a Christian Nation Again?* (Ft. Lauderdale: Coral Ridge Ministries, 2003), a video.

318 William J. Federer, *America's God and Country* (St. Louis: Amerisearch, 2000), 319.

319 Speech in the Virginia Convention, 5 June, 1788; *Complete Madison*, 46, Caroline Thomas Harnsberger, ed., *Treasury of Presidential Quotations* (Chicago: Follett Publishing Company, 1964), 107.

320 Jim Davis, "'Duty is ours; results are God's'" *Sun-Sentinel*, http://www.sun-sentinel.com/features/religion/faith-and-values/fl-fv-qa-jerry-20110602,0,262093.story.

321 John Eidsmoe, *Christianity and the Constitution* (Grand Rapids: Baker Book House, 1987), 170.

INDEX OF
PROPER NAMES

NOTES

NOTES

NOTES

NOTES

NOTES

NOTES